A COLLECTION OF
Indo-global recipes
BOOK 4 CODA & MISCELLANEOUS RECIPES

BY IRA GHOSH

BLUEROSE PUBLISHERS
India | U.K.

Copyright © Ira Ghosh 2025

All rights reserved by author. No part of this publication may be reproduced, stored in a retrieval system or transmitted in any form or by any means, electronic, mechanical, photocopying, recording or otherwise, without the prior permission of the author. Although every precaution has been taken to verify the accuracy of the information contained herein, the publisher assumes no responsibility for any errors or omissions. No liability is assumed for damages that may result from the use of information contained within.

BlueRose Publishers takes no responsibility for any damages, losses, or liabilities that may arise from the use or misuse of the information, products, or services provided in this publication.

For permissions requests or inquiries regarding this publication,
please contact:

BLUEROSE PUBLISHERS
www.BlueRoseONE.com
info@bluerosepublishers.com
+91 8882 898 898
+4407342408967

ISBN: 978-93-6452-673-9

Cover design: Yash Singhal
Typesetting: Namrata Saini

First Edition: February 2025

Dedication

I dedicate this book to my late husband Ashis Bindu Ghosh. When we married, I could barely cook! However, my culinary abilities grew and flourished through his constant encouragement and support (and unfailing good humour at some of my less successful creations). His career enabled us to live in different countries and experience and appreciate different cultures. Much later, after I had accumulated my varied collection of recipes from around the world, he encouraged me to share them through their publication. He was instrumental in getting the first version of my recipe collection into a publishable form. If it were not for his hard work, support, and encouragement, this book would not exist, and I would not have been able to share my recipe collection with you.

I also dedicate this book to my mother Ratnavali Baruah who was a very good cook and had some fantastic recipes. She however, never had any set formula. Before my marriage my mother always worried about my lack of culinary ability!

Additionally, I dedicate this book to my grandmother Pragna Sundari Devi who was the first person to author a series of systematic cookbooks in Bengali extending to several volumes. Her books were my constant reference abroad, from which I learnt my basics.

TABLE OF CONTENTS

Introduction 1
Weights, Measures, And Temperatures 3

PASTRIES, PIES, AND PANCAKES 7
Phyllo Or Filo Pastry (Middle Eastern) 9
Flaky Pastry 10
Basic Short Crust Pastry 11
Yorkshire Pudding 12
Pakhlava 13
Beorek (I) 14
Beorek (II) 15
Beorek (III) 16
Corn Pie 17
Spinach Pie 18
Cocktail Or Tea Puffs 19
Delicious Creamcheese Pie (I) 20
Creamcheese Pie (Ii) 21
Criss Cross Linzer 22
Brandy Snaps Made Easy 23
Donut 24
Czech Fritters 25
German Apple Fritters 26
Quick Economic Apple Pancakes 27
Chinese Fritter Batter 28
Indian Black Berry (Kaala Jaam) Tart 29
Guava Pie 30
Soya Bean Pie 32
Banana Pancakes 33
Cottage Cheese Pancakes 34
Chocolate Pancake Dessert 35
Dalia Or Borgul Malpua (Cracked Wheat Pancakes) 36
Czech Apple Strűdel 37
Fruit Waffles/Fritters/Pancakes 38
Dárazsfeszek – (Hungarian Sweet Pastry) 39

Langosh 40
Cheesecake 41
Basic Scones 42
Cheese Scones 43
Guyanese Rich Coconut Bens 44

TEATIME AND COCKTAIL SNACKS 45

Cheese Snacks 47
Cheese Pakoras 48
Cheese Balls 49
Sago Bhujia 50
Japanese Beans Rolled In Pork 51
Methi (Fenugreek) Straws 52
Potato Crisps 53
Preserved Potatoes Chips 54
Chuchurbawang 55
Surprise Potatoes 56
Bhakari Vadi 58
Placky Or Czech Savory Potato Pancakes 59
Clam Canapés 60
Clam Dip 61
Olive And Bacon Canapés 62
Cocktail Tid Bits 63
Stuffed Dill Pickle 64
Apple And Roquefort Cheese 65
Anchovy Puff 66
Liver Paté 67
Liver And Pork Paté 68
Falafel 69
Dalia Pakora (Cracked Wheat Or Borgul Balls) 71
Rice Cakes Or Pakoras 72
Katjang Mana Lagi (Indonesian Peanut Brittle) 73
Rempejek* (Indonesian Peanut Chips) 74
Luncheon Meat Koftas 75
Mince Kebabs 76
Egg Kebab 77

Egyptian Kabeba 78
Quick Kebabs Or Koftas 79
Mowcha Or Banana Flower Koftas 80
Mowcha (Banana Flower) Kebabs 82
Kanchkala Or Green Banana Burgers 83
Sausage Rolls 84
Rolls From Left-Over Mince Curry 86
Savoury Rolls 87
Cottage Cheese Ham Rolls 88
Piquant Sausages 89
Chicken Chaat 90
Savory Sesame Machine Biscuits 91
Savory Peanut Biscuits 92
Salty Biscuits 93
Savoury Biscuits 94
Lahnmahajan Or Lebanese Pizza 95
Lahmedjun (Armenian Pizzas) 97
Crumb-Fried Or Batter-Fried Roe 98
Fish Wafers 99
Prawn Snacks 100
Crumb-Fried Or Batter-Fried Cottage Cheese 101
Battered Bread Snacks 102
Flavoured Cottage/Cream Cheese On Toast 103
Cottage Cheese Paneer Spread 105
Cottage Cheese Snacks 106
Khasta Fish Puffs 107
Fish Katchuri 109
Khasta Singara 110

JAMS, PICKLES, SQUASHES, AND SAUCES 111

Simple Quick Easy Orange Marmalade 113
Gooseberry Jam (I) 114
Gooseberry Jam (II) 115
Pear Jam 116
Pineapple Jam (I) 117
Pineapple Jam (II) 118

Guava Jelly 119
Guava Cheese 120
Peanut Butter 121
Lemon Ginger Juice 122
Wood Apple (*Baël*) Squash 123
Pineapple Squash 124
Quick White Sauce 125
Easy Brown Sauce 126
Tahina Sauce (Middle Eastern) 127
Beer Syrup 128
Mock Cream 129
Mock Sour Cream 130
Dessert Sauces 131
Catsup 133
Tomato Purée 134
Tomato Chutney 135
Kharisa (Assamese Bamboo Shoot Pickle) 136
Pork Pickle 137
Mummy's Vindaloo Or Meat Pickle 138

MISCELLANEOUS RECIPES **139**

Sangria (I) 141
Batida De Limao (Brazilian Drink) 142
Glögg (Swedish Hot Christmas Drink) 143
South Indian Lassi 144
Feijoada Paulista (Brazilian Dish) 145
Pancake Party 147
Hungarian Savoury Dish 150
Idli Or South Indian Steam-Buns 151
Dosa (South Indian Stuffed Pancakes) 152
Semolina Dosa (South Indian Pancakes) 154
Arrowroot Dosas Or South Indian Pancakes 155
All In One Dish 156
Recycling Left-Over Tandoori Roti Or Chapattis 157
Finnish Cabbage Pie 158
Karelian Steak 159

Koubbeh (Lebanese National Dish) 160
Spring Rolls (I) 161
Chinese Spring Rolls (Ii) 163
Indonesian Spring Rolls The Easy Way 164
Sushi 166
Tamagodofu (Japanese) 167
Chop Suey 168
Oriental Meat Loaf 169
Sukiyaki 170
Fuyong Hai (Indonesian) 171
Oopuma (Savoury Semolina Dish From South India) 172
Cabbage Scramble Eggs 173
Scrambled Cabbage With Left-Over Meat 174
Left-Over From Left-Overs! 175
Preserving Vegetables 176
Radish Flower 177
Stuffed Batter Fried Patal/Palwal (Indian Vegetable) 178
Salad Platter 180
Cheese Soufflé 181
Ground Meat, Chicken Or Fish Pie 182
Quick Hamburgers 183
Quick And Easy Pizza 184
Mock Lasagne 185
Dalia Porridge 187
Granola 188
Chocolate 189

Glossary 190
Alphabetical List of Recipes 195

INTRODUCTION

"*A Collection of Indo Global Recipes*", as the name suggests, is a collection of recipes that is influenced by my Indian background, as well as being the result of spending many years in different countries where my husband's job took me. While abroad, I actively participated in various international groups and made friends with people from many different countries.

I do not consider myself a great cook! However, I was always interested in collecting and devising new recipes and trying them out on friends and family. Their enthusiastic responses indicated that I must have been doing something right! Hoping that others might wish to enjoy the pleasure of cooking and experimenting with recipes from around the world with minimum effort, I decided to publish my collection. In addition to many of the Indian recipes I inherited or learned from my family, I have been building this collection since my husband's first international posting in 1967. I have also added to the collection recipes that I invented over this time. I have tried out all the recipes, and this book is the result of my explorations, collection, and experimentation. Many of the recipes have familiar names, but often prepared differently by various cooks. I tried to simplify each recipe, and in doing so built up a collection that is user-friendly. In a few recipes I could not forgo the temptation of using "ajinomoto" (MSG; monosodium glutamate) as this was a popular ingredient when I collected the recipes. In the intervening years, it was reputed to be harmful, but recently it has been classified by the U.S. Food and Drug Administration of being safe. However, if there is concern, ajinomoto may be replaced with a pinch of sugar to retain somewhat similar flavour.

I hope my work will be of use to many enthusiastic and curious cooks including the offspring of Indian diaspora living abroad, youthful techies wishing to serve party-fares, connoisseurs researching ethnic cooking, and adventurous cooks wanting to make good, interesting food with ease from diverse recipes. Some of the dishes remain time-consuming, but most can be made with a few quick and easy steps.

This book was a labour of love, and my family encouraged me through the years I took to complete this project. I published the first version of this collection, entitled "*A Collection of Recipes*" in 2012 in one large volume. My husband did the tremendous job of computerization and editing that version. However, before I could publish my book, I needed to first complete another important project. I had taken on the colossal task of editing the multi-volume cookbook in Bengali titled "*Amish O Niramish Ahar*" written by my grandmother Pragna Sundari Devi. My grandmother was the first writer of a systematic cookbook in Bengali. Her volumes were published starting from the year 1900 AD. My re-edited and re-arranged versions were published in 1995, after which I could concentrate on my recipe collection. In the years since I first published my collection, I have received feedback and added to it. It is now timely to re-edit and publish the current collection, but this time as a four-volume set to make it more accessible, user friendly, and with a slight change in title to reflect its roots in both Indian and international cuisines. My son, Dr. Richik Niloy Ghosh, was instrumental in helping me create this new four-volume version.

Many thanks are due to my relations and friends in India and abroad from whom I collected the original recipes, modified versions of which now appear in these pages. I am unable to thank them all individually. As my sources were from many nationalities using various units of measurements (metric, avoirdupois, and cups), I kept the units as were given in the originals. To assist the users, I have appended a conversion table covering the three systems. A glossary has also been added to help the reader to understand unfamiliar terms.

Bon Appétit

Ira Ghosh

29 February 2024

WEIGHTS, MEASURES, and TEMPERATURES

1. SOLID MEASURES

1 kg. (kilogram) = 1,000 gm. (gram) = 2.2 lb. (pound avoirdupois)

1 lb. = 16 oz. (ounce)

(a) Equivalent measures of some commodities

Avoirdupois measure	Commodity	Container equivalent
1 pound	Butter or other fat	2 cups
1 pound	Flour	4 cups
1 pound	Granulated or castor sugar	2 cups
1 pound	Icing or confectioner's sugar	3 cups
1 pound	Brown (moist) sugar	2 cups
1 pound	Golden syrup or treacle	1 cup
1 pound	Rice	2 cups
1 pound	Dried fruit	2 cups
1 pound	Chopped meat (finely packed)	2 cups
1 pound	Lentils or split peas	2 cups
1 pound	Coffee (beans)	2 cups
1 pound	Soft breadcrumbs	4 cups
½ ounce	Flour	1 level tablespoon
1 ounce	Flour	1 heaped tablespoon
1 ounce	Sugar	1 level tablespoon
¾ ounce	Butter	1 tablespoon smoothed off
1 ounce	Golden syrup or treacle	1 tablespoon
1 ounce	Jam or jelly	1 level tablespoon

(b) Dry volume/ weight measures

Container	Container	Volume	Weight
4 teaspoons (tsp.)	1 tablespoon	½ fluid ounce	14.3 grams
2 tablespoons (tblsp.)	⅛ cup	1 fluid ounce	28.6 grams
4 tablespoons	⅓ cup	2 fluid ounces	56.7 grams
5⅓ tablespoons	½ cup	2.6 fluid ounce	75.6 grams
8 tablespoons	½ cup	4 fluid ounces	113.4 grams
12 tablespoons	¾ cup	6 fluid ounces	170 grams (.375 pound)
32 tablespoons	2 cups	16 fluid ounces	453.6 grams (1 Pound)
64 tablespoons	4 cups	32 fluid ounces	907 grams (2 pounds)

2. LIQUID MEASURES

(a) Common usage

Measure	Measure	Measure	Volume
1 cup	8 fluid ounces	½ pint	237 millilitres
2 cups	16 fluid ounces	1 pint	474 millilitres.
4 cups	32 fluid ounces	1 quart	946 millilitres
1 pint	16 fluid ounces	½ quart	473 millilitres
2 pints	32 fluid ounces	1 quart	0.964 litres.
4 quarts	128 fluid ounces	1 gallon	3.784 litres
8 quarts	One peck		
4 pecks	One bushel		
dash	Less than ¼ teaspoon		

(b) Small quantities

1 teaspoon (US)	1/6 ounce	4.93 millilitres
1 tablespoon (US)	0.5 ounce	3 teaspoons
1 teaspoon (UK)	1.2 teaspoon (US)	6.16 millilitres
1 tablespoon (UK)	1.2 tablespoon (US)	18.48 millilitres
1 dessert spoon (UK)	2.4 teaspoons	12.32 millilitres
1 dash	~ ⅛ teaspoon	~ 0.6 millilitres

3. APPROXIMATE OVEN TEMPERATURES

Oven	Gas Regulo	Electricity	
		°F	°C
Cool	0 - ½	225 – 250	107 – 121
Very Slow	½ - 1	250 – 275	121 -135
Slow	1 - 2	275 – 300	135 – 149
Very Moderate	2 – 3	300 – 350	149 – 177
Moderate	4	375	190
Moderately Hot	5	400	204
Hot	6 – 7	435 – 450	218 – 233
Very Hot	8 - 9	475 - 500	245 - 260

Ovens might somewhat differ in their specifications.

PASTRIES, PIES, AND PANCAKES

PHYLLO OR FILO PASTRY (MIDDLE EASTERN)

8 oz. floor   ½ tsp. baking powder

Water for mixing

Method

Sift flour and baking powder. Mix enough water gradually to make a stiff dough. Should not be too soft or dry or elastic. Great care should be taken in adding the water. Cover dough and let it rest for 2 hours. Take off bits of dough the size of tennis balls and roll paper thin. Now use for your favourite recipes.

FLAKY PASTRY

6 oz, flour

1 tsp. salt or to taste

Ice water as required

3 oz. margarine/butter

Method

Sift flour and salt together. Add enough ice water to make a pliable dough. Shape Into an oblong and roll out. Dot centre of dough with the shortening or spread with a knife. Fold the dry section of the dough from the top over the shortening and then fold over with the lower section of the dry dough. In other words, fold in three. Seal the edges. Repeat this three times. Place in the refrigerator for 20-30 minutes in between each rolling.

This pastry can be used to cover any savoury or sweet pie and then baked in a hot oven.

Rolled Pasties / Patties:

To make small *Rolled Pasties/Patties* cut pastry with a cup. Brush surface generously with milk to make it stick. Place filling on the top end (not too much or else it will spill out) and fold over with the second half of the pastry like a curry puff or half-moon shape. Seal and crimple edges. Bake in a hot oven till pastry is brown and done. Serve with any pickle /chutney or sauce.

Filling

Hard boiled eggs chopped small, peeled, and thinly sliced tomatoes and grated cheese. Place them on the pastry in the order given

Alternately any other meat / fish /chicken filling can be used with spices or mixed in a thick white/ cheese/ tomato sauce as per choice.

A good tea-time or cocktail snack.

BASIC SHORT CRUST PASTRY

8 oz. flour

4 oz. butter, or ½ butter and ½ any shortening

Ice water as required

Method

All the ingredients must be cold. In a bowl, cut the butter into the flour with two knives till the whole resembles breadcrumbs. Gradually sprinkle ice-water and continue mixing with a wooden spoon till mixture forms into a ball and does not stick to the side of the bowl. If possible, avoid using hand for mixing this dough. Leave dough in the refrigerator till required.

Note:

If the dough is used to make a savoury dish, sift 1 tsp. salt with the flour. For any sweet dish, 1 tblsp. powdered or castor sugar could be mixed with the flour.

YORKSHIRE PUDDING

1½ oz. flour

1 large egg

2 tblsp. any shortening

Salt to taste

Ice water and milk, as required

Method

Sift flour and salt together. Add the egg and sufficient ice water to form a paste like Consistency. Beat with a wooden spoon or a hand blender. Pour in some milk and continue to beat. It should be of a thick pouring consistency. Put ½ tsp shortening in 4 Yorkshire pudding patty pans or any other wide flat patty pans. Heat pans in the oven to melt shortening. Take pans out of the oven and pour mixture into them. Bake in the top rack of a hot oven till top is brown. Gently lift out of pans and serve with roast beef. The Yorkshire pudding can also be poured into a single medium shallow pie pan. When ready it can be cut into serving pieces.

PAKHLAVA

(This Middle Eastern sweet is not for those who do not have a sweet tooth!)

1 kg. walnuts before shelling	½ cup sugar
1 tsp. cinnamon powder	½ kg. *'filo or phyllo'* **pastry – 2 sheets
¼ kg. margarine melted	

See under "Pastries" section of this book

Method

Shell, clean and grind walnuts. Add sugar and cinnamon, and mix. Sprinkle walnut mixture on 2 *filo* sheets. Roll each and press till the sheet crinkles. Cut up in small slices and place on baking sheet. Pour margarine generously over the slices. (If necessary, add a little more melted margarine). Bake in a moderate oven till brown. Pour warm sugar syrup over *Pakhlava* and serve.

Variation:

Brush one filo sheet with a generous amount of margarine. Spread walnut mixture over it. Cover with the second sheet of filo. Cut in squares and place on a baking tray. Pour the rest of the margarine over it. Use a little more melted margarine if necessary. Bake and continue as above.

Sugar Syrup

2 cups sugar	1 cup water
1 tsp. fresh lemon juice	

Bring sugar and water to boil. Let boil for about 3-4 minutes. Take off heat and add lemon juice. Pour over pakhlava.

BEOREK (I)

1 cup cream cheese
1 tblsp. parsley chopped
¼ kg. margarine melted

1 large egg
½ kg. (2 sheets) *filo**

Method

Mix cheese, egg, and parsley. Spread mixture on top of *filo* sheets. Roll up and press till pastry crinkles. Cut in slices. Pour margarine over slices and place on a baking tray. Bake in a moderate oven till golden. Serve warm.

Variation:

Brush one *filo* sheet with half the margarine. Spread cheese mixture over it. Place second sheet over the filling. Pour rest of margarine over it. Use a little more melted margarine if necessary. Now cut and proceed baking as above. This is an easier way of assembling the beorek.

BEOREK (II)

1-1/3 cup heaped flour

½ tsp. salt

4 eggs

6 oz. (more or less) feta, cottage or similar cheese cut in thick slices and then into fingers

1 tsp. baking powder

2 cups (more or less) oil

Water as required

Method

Sift flour, baking powder and salt in a large bowl. Make a well in the centre and pour 1½ tblsp. oil into it. Beat the eggs one at a time into the well with a fork and very gradually add the flour from the sides. At the same time keep adding water a little at a time. When the flour, oil and eggs are slightly mixed knead dough well adding extra flour as well as water if required, all a little at a time. A lot of kneading is necessary until dough is soft. Divide dough into 2-3 or more sections. Roll out each section very thin. Sprinkle cheese fingers with salt if unsalted. Lay the fingers on the rolled-out dough width wise singly or in 2 to 3 in a row. Now cut the dough to the width size of the cheese. Roll the cheese in each strip of dough 3 times and then cut off. Seal the edges securely with a fork. Deep fry in oil. Drain on paper towel. Serve hot with ketchup or any other sauce of choice.

Altogether, about 1 lb flour has been used for the dough. Feta cheese is best suited for this recipe.

BEOREK (III)

6 eggs	1 cup milk
150 gm. butter	500 gm. *filo* pastry
1 kg. shortening or, 1 litre oil or, as much as required	450 gm. any white cheese
Salt, only if required depending on the saltiness of the cheese	3 tblsp. chopped parsley
Pepper to taste (optional)	

Method

Beat the eggs well. Warm milk and butter together. When the butter melts add the eggs beating continuously to mix. Make sure the mixture does not curdle. Keep aside. Grease an oblong baking sheet and line it with a thin sheet of *filo* pastry. Brush *filo* sheet generously with melted shortening. Place another thin filo sheet on top and brush this with the egg mixture. Continue in this way till it reaches a thickness of 1"-1½" or till one half of the *filo* sheets are used up. Mix the cheese, parsley and seasoning if using. Spread this mixture evenly over the last filo sheet. Cover with another filo sheet. Now continue as before alternating with melted shortening and egg mixture till the rest of the *filo* sheets are all used up. Cover the top filo sheet with egg mixture and pierce in several places with a sharp knife. Bake in a moderately hot oven till the top is a golden colour. Remove from the oven and cut in squares. Serve hot with a green salad or by itself as a snack.

CORN PIE

8 oz. short crust pastry

8 oz. fresh corn or, canned creamed corn or kernels

Salt and pepper to taste

½ cup milk

1 small green pepper minced

1 tblsp. breadcrumbs

2 eggs

1-2 tblsp. butter

2 large onions minced

2-4 slices bacon minced

Method

Line an 8" pastry tin with the pastry evenly. Sprinkle base of pastry with breadcrumbs. Mix all the other ingredients together and cover pastry shell with it. Bake in a hot oven for 30–45 minutes or till set and pastry is cooked. Serve hot cut in wedges. If using fresh corn, boil in water and then put in the blender or food processor before mixing with the other ingredients. For canned corn kernels no need to boil. Just put in the blender or food processor and continue as above.

SPINACH PIE

3-4 eggs	250 gm. feta cheese crumbled
2 medium onions chopped	8 tblsp. olive oil/melted butter
1 kg. spinach	1 tblsp. fresh dill/parsley leaves chopped
Salt and pepper to taste	½-1 tsp. nutmeg grated
2 tblsp. parmesan/any other cheese grated	400-500 gm. filo pastry sheets

Method

Mix the egg with the feta cheese. Keep aside. Sauté onion lightly in oil. Add the spinach and sauté a little more. Next add parsley or dill. Now add seasoning and nutmeg. Stir before adding the egg mixture. Keep stirring to mix on low heat. Remove from heat. Sprinkle with the cheese and gently stir to mix. Grease an oven - proof dish and line with 8-10 filo sheets. Brush each sheet with melted butter. Spread the spinach filling evenly over the sheets. Cover with another 8–10 sheets brushing each sheet with melted butter. Turn down the edges and brush top, sides, and edges with butter. Cut into shapes. Bake in a med. hot oven for about ½ hour or till top is golden. Serve hot as a snack or an accompaniment with any meat dish.

Variation:

The spinach can be substituted with brain cooked in bechamel sauce or cooked ground meat with any seasoning according to taste.

COCKTAIL or TEA PUFFS

Method

Roll out any left-over short crust pastry very thin. Cut in small rounds. Lightly spread each cut out pastry with any jam/jelly, pea-nut butter, or chocolate/orange/lemon spread or filling etc. for a sweet puff. Alternately spread the cut-out pastry with any, of the following for savoury puffs: any pâté, paste, sandwich filling e.g. sardines, tuna, salmon, herrings, anchovies, cheese, luncheon meat, corned beef etc.

If necessary, soften the cheese or any of the fish with anchovy or fish sauce and ketchup or Worcester sauce or any other sauce of choice. Fold the puffs over once in half to form a ½ moon shape. Brush tops with either egg yolk or milk. Lay them carefully on a greased and floured baking sheet and bake in a hot oven for about 10–5 minutes or till done – a golden colour. They should be crisp.

DELICIOUS CREAMCHEESE PIE (I)

Filling:

1 litre milk or 500 gm. cottage cheese

2 tblsp. sugar

2 tblsp. raisins

1 egg

1 tsp. vanilla essence

Method

If using fresh milk, keep the bottle or packet outside (not in the refrigerator) unopened for 48 hours. Next day warm the milk but do not boil. When milk starts to curdle take off heat and cool. Strain through a cheese cloth. Add all the above ingredients and mix well.

Pastry:

1 lb. flour

5 tblsp. un-softened margarine or butter

1 tsp. grated lemon rind

1 tsp. baking powder

1 tblsp. sugar

2-3 eggs or more, if required

Sift flour and baking powder together. Add margarine or butter and mix till like breadcrumbs. Now add the sugar and lemon rind and mix thoroughly but without kneading. Last of all add the eggs one by one to bind the dough. No other liquid should be used. This dough should not be kneaded at all or handled too much. A quick assembling of the ingredients will produce best results. No need to roll. Reserve ¼ of the dough. Just pat the rest of the dough with hands and line a greased and floured round pie tin bringing pastry up the sides of the tin evenly.

Assembly:

Sprinkle breadcrumbs or semolina on the base of the pastry. Put the filling on top of this. From the ¼ reserved dough put a little (approx. 1 tblsp) aside. Place the rest of the dough on top of the filling completely covering it evenly. Now make long thin strips out of the 1 tblsp dough kept aside and place on the top of the pie in a crisscross or any other pattern. Brush with cold milk. Bake in a moderately hot oven for about ½ hr or till top is a golden colour.

CREAMCHEESE PIE (II)

Pastry:

10 oz. flour

2 tblsp. sugar

3 egg yolks

2 tsp. baking powder

4 oz. margarine or butter

Method

Sift flour and baking powder together. Add sugar and then margarine and butter. Mix well till like breadcrumbs. Add egg yolks one at a time and mix to bind dough as no other liquid is to be added. Do not handle the dough more than necessary and try to assemble it as quickly as possible. Pat dough down with hands. Do not roll. Line a greased and floured round pie tin with the dough bringing it up the sides evenly. Sprinkle base with semolina or breadcrumbs.

Filling:

1½ litre fresh milk

3 egg yolks

10 gm. sugar

2 tsp. vanilla essence

Make cream cheese out of milk as given in "Cream Cheese Pie (I)". When cold add the sugar, egg yolks and vanilla and mix well. Place the filling into the unbaked pie shell. Bake in hot oven 450°F till done about 20 minutes.

Meringue:

6 egg whites

6 tblsp. castor or, powdered sugar

2 tblsp. any jam

Beat egg whites and jam together till almost stiff. Add sugar gradually by one tablespoon at a time. Take pie out of the oven and spread meringue evenly over it. Return to oven and bake for another 20 minutes. Reduce heat to 200°.F or medium low and continue to bake for approximately another 30 minutes or till meringue is brown but not burnt.

CRISS CROSS LINZER

500 gm. flour	2 tsp. baking powder
13 oz. margarine	10 oz. icing sugar
5 oz. any nut powdered (optional)	½ tsp. or more cinnamon powder
½ tsp. grated lemon rind	1 egg
4 oz. fresh milk or, 1 tblsp. fresh cream	Any flavoured jam to spread on pastry

Method

Sift flour and baking powder. Rub in margarine. Add sugar, nuts, cinnamon, lemon rind, egg, and milk. Mix all quickly like short pastry. Rest in refrigerator for about ½ hour. Roll out 2/3 of the pastry to fit a greased and floured rectangular baking tray. Spread jam liberally over the pastry. Roll remainder of the 1/3 pastry and cut into narrow strips. Lay these strips over the jam pastry in a crisscross design. Brush with egg or milk or egg white and milk combination. Bake in moderately hot oven for about 20-25 minutes.

BRANDY SNAPS MADE EASY

2 oz. butter or margarine

2 oz. golden syrup

2 oz. flour sifted

½ tsp. or more finely grated lemon rind

2 oz. brown sugar

½ tsp. ginger powder

½ tsp. lemon juice

Fresh thick cream as required

Method

In a saucepan warm gently, on very low heat, butter, sugar, syrup, and ginger till butter melts and all well mixed. Take off heat. Gradually add flour, lemon juice and rind. Mix all well. Grease a cookie sheet well. Drop batter by a teaspoon in rounds on the sheet well apart from each other. Bake in a pre-heated moderate oven (325) for about 5 minutes or till done.

Take out from the oven and roll each very quickly around the handle of a wooden spoon. It may be difficult to roll the brandy snaps straight from the oven as they could be a little soft for rolling. So, wait till just right. This requires a little experience and practice!! Kept out too long again could make them too hard to roll. They should be ready for rolling after a few seconds of coming out from the oven. In case they become too hard for rolling put them back in the oven for a couple of minutes. When all have been rolled fill them with fresh cream. Sprinkle with icing sugar – optional.

DONUT

3 tsp. yeast	1 kg. flour sifted
3 egg yolks	1½ pt. (approx.) milk
3 tblsp. butter/margarine melted	1½ cup (approx.) oil for frying
Cinnamon or vanillin sugar for spreading on top	Any jam filling (if desired)

Method

Mix yeast with 1-2 tsp sugar and a little warm milk just to cover and set aside to form bubbles and rise. If the yeast is active this process should take just a few minutes. Put the flour in a large wide bowl. Make a well in the centre of the flour and add the yeast and egg yolks. Mix all well by drawing the flour into the centre gradually. Add just enough milk to make a soft dough. Knead either in the food processor or by hands. Add the melted butter gradually in the processor or put on hands while kneading. Cover with a cloth and leave to rise in a warm place for 1½ hours or till dough is double the original size. Roll dough on a floured board ¼" thick. Cut in approximately 2½" diameter and leave to rise for another ½ hour. or a little more. (If desired another small round may be cut into the centre of the doughnuts). If the doughnuts are left whole, then make a deep depression in the centre with the thumb. Warm oil and deep fry. Drain on paper towels and dredge with any flavour sugar of your choice. Alternately the doughnut may be split in half and sandwiched with jam and then the top sprinkled with icing, castor, or powdered sugar.

Variation:

Many prefer to put a savoury or sweetened cream or cottage cheese filling in the centre of the doughnuts and then fry them. In such cases be sure to cover the filling well so they do not spill out while frying.

CZECH FRITTERS

3 tsp. dry yeast, or 10 oz. fresh yeast

½ litre milk

2 large eggs separated

6 oz. sugar

20 oz. flour

Oil for frying

Method

In a bowl mix yeast with 1 heaped tsp. sugar. Add a little warm (not too hot) milk just enough to cover the yeast/sugar. Keep in warm place to form bubbles and rise. Sift flour in another large bowl and make a hollow in the centre. Put egg yolks, rest of the milk and sugar and 2 tsp of oil in the hollow. Draw the flour into the hollow slowly from the sides and mix all well. Add the yeast mixture, mix, and then beat manually or with an electric beater for about 10 minutes. Let dough rest covered for about 45 minutes. Beat egg whites stiff and fold into the dough. Rest for another 10 minutes. Warm oil in a deep fry pan. Do not make the oil too hot or else the fritters will brown quickly on the outside and remain uncooked inside. Dip a round soup spoon in oil and then lift batter and drop gently into the warmed oil. Fry the fritters in batches depending on the size of the pan. Keep stirring to brown evenly. If the oil becomes too hot, take off from direct heat and keep aside for a while but continue to fry the fritters. When the oil becomes cold, return pan to direct heat. Slow frying of the fritters will produce better results. Drain off oil from fritters on paper towel. Sprinkle with powdered castor sugar. Serve with butter or jam.

GERMAN APPLE FRITTERS

1 tblsp. heaped flour sifted	A dash of salt
1-2 tsp. sugar	1 egg
2-4 tblsp. beer (more or less)	2 medium apples sliced
Oil for deep frying	1-2 tsp. vanillin sugar/cinnamon powder

Method

Mix all the dry ingredients except vanillin sugar together. Add the egg slightly beaten and stir. Now add enough beer to make a fritter batter of the right consistency. It should not be too thin. Drop the apple slices into the batter and stir gently to coat. Heat oil and fry apple slices in small batches till golden and crisp. Sprinkle with vanillin sugar or cinnamon powder and serve immediately while still hot. Custard or fresh cream can be served as an accompaniment.

QUICK ECONOMIC APPLE PANCAKES

Batter:

4 oz. flour	1 tsp. baking powder or, 1 egg slightly beaten
1 tblsp. melted butter	Sufficient liquid for the batter (milk/water/left over soda or beer is a good option)
1 tblsp. sugar	

Mix all the above together to form batter consistency. Keep aside

Filling:

1 apple chopped	2 tblsp. brown sugar
¼ tsp. cinnamon powder	¼ tsp. nutmeg powder
1-2 tblsp. raisins (optional)	2 tblsp. corn flour

Mix all the filling ingredients together and keep aside till required.

Method

Brush a heavy- bottomed griddle or non-stick fry pan with oil. Drop batter with a medium round spoon and tilt pan to spread. When bubbles appear and pancake is slightly set place filling in the middle spreading with the back of spoon. Fold pancake in three like a triangle. Turn over and cook for a few seconds gently pressing down with a spoon. Take off heat and keep warm till all the batter and filling are done. Sprinkle pancakes slightly with lemon juice a little before serving. Next, sprinkle with icing sugar just before serving.

CHINESE FRITTER BATTER

1 egg
Ice cubes/cold water

Flour as required

Method

Break the egg in a bowl and stir without beating. Add flour as required. Add enough water to get a light batter consistency. Let rest for a while – 15-20 minutes or more. Marinate shrimps, chicken, lamb/beef strips etc. in a combination of soya sauce, garlic and ginger powder or juice for ½ hour and then dip in the batter and deep fry. Drain on paper towel before serving. Serve with extra soya sauce, chilli sauce, peanut sauce etc. etc. Strips of vegetables e.g. carrots, green beans etc. or fruit slices e.g. apple, orange, pear etc. can also be dipped in the batter and fried like the meats. Serve fruit sprinkled with powdered sugar and cream if desired. This is a very light batter and need not be used as a thick coating.

INDIAN BLACK BERRY (KAALA JAAM) TART

(*Kaala jaam* is supposed to be good for those with a sugar problem. However, the following delicious and unusual recipe has no guarantee to benefit those with a high sugar problem!)

12 oz. sifted flour	2 tblsp. granulated sugar
1-2 eggs	6 oz. butter/margarine or any other shortening
¼ cup or more iced water or, cold milk as required	

Method

Sift flour and sugar. Add egg and mix. Add the shortening and mix lightly till dough resembles breadcrumbs. Add water/milk or half and half gradually mixing with a wooden spoon till dough forms a soft ball. Cover with wax paper and store in the refrigerator till required.

Filling:

2 lbs kaala jaam soaked in ½ cup lime juice and ½ tsp heaped baking soda for 1-2 hrs or more to get the acidity of the berries out. Wash thoroughly and pressure cook with a little water. When cold mash thoroughly taking the seeds out. Now make a thick jam with the berries.

Jam:

1 lb. sugar	2-4 tblsp. lime juice
½ cup raisins	1 tsp. each ginger and cinnamon powder or, 1 tsp. mixed spice

Mix all the above ingredients with the berries and cook over medium heat constantly stirring till resembles a thickish jam. Taste for sweetness.

Grease and flour a pie tin. Roll dough to shape and gently line pie tin with it. Sprinkle breadcrumbs over it. Place in a moderate oven and half bake. – 10-15 minutes. Take out and fill with jam. Cut strips with any left-over dough and place over jam in a crisscross fashion. Bake in the oven again till done. Cut in squares and serve plain for tea or with fresh cream as a dessert.

GUAVA PIE

8 oz. flour	2 tblsp. sugar powdered
4 oz. butter	2 egg yolks
Ice cold water (optional)	

Method

Sift dry ingredients together. Add the butter and mix till resembles breadcrumbs. Add the eggs and keep mixing till dough is soft and pliable. If necessary, only then add ice cold water. Dough should not be too dry or too sticky. Roll out dough to a round shape to ¼" thickness. Line a well-greased and floured round pie pan with the pastry. Prick the base with a fork. Sprinkle breadcrumbs on top and then bake in a hot oven for 15-20 minutes. Fill pie shell to the top with the guava jam. Pile meringue on top of the guava pie and bake in a moderate oven for 20-30 minutes or till the meringue browns. Serve cut in slices with fresh cream or vanilla ice cream

Filling:

1 kg. guavas	500 gm. sugar (more or less depending on the sweetness of the fruit)
1 tblsp. lime juice	

Cut guavas into small pieces, sprinkle with lime juice and then pressure cook for about 5 minutes. When cool put in the blender or a food processor. Stir in the sugar and cook on low heat, if necessary, to dry off any excess liquid. It should be of a jam consistency.

Meringue:

4 egg whites	2 tblsp. icing sugar sieved

Beat the egg whites stiff. Fold in the icing sugar gradually and keep beating.

Variation:

Use the pulp left over from making guava jelly or guava jam. Put the pulp in the food processor and process for a few minutes till the pulp is smooth and the seeds are totally broken down. Mix 4 tblsp. sugar and a little lime juice with it before filling in the pie crust. This is a more economical way of making the pie and the pulp does not need any extra cooking. It is also equally delicious!

SOYA BEAN PIE

Method

Pie Crust:

Follow the same method as for the 'guava pie'.

Filling:

1 cup soya bean soaked over night	3 egg yolks
½ cup (approx.) milk	8 tblsp heaped sugar
½ tsp each ginger, cinnamon, nutmeg powder	1 tsp vanilla essence

Wash the soya beans several times in cold water to get rid of the skins. Puree the beans in a blender or food processor. Mix with all the other ingredients and cook on low heat till thick. Keep stirring continuously during cooking making sure not to let the mixture curdle. Leave to cool.

Meringue:

2 egg whites	2 tblsp. icing sugar
A pinch of cream of tartar	

Beat egg whites stiff. Add the sugar and cream of tartar and continue to beat.

Spread the soya bean filling into the pie crust evenly. Cover with the meringue while still stiff. Bake in a hot oven till the pie is set and the top is golden brown.

Variation:

Instead of using the spice powders and vanilla essence substitute with 1 tsp. of thin slivers of almond and 1 tsp. of almond essence. Other flavourings such as clove or cardamom powder, lemon, strawberry, orange, chocolate, coffee or a combination of chocolate and coffee to get a mocha flavour etc. etc. could also be substituted.

BANANA PANCAKES

3 eggs

3-5 mashed ripe bananas

1 tsp. oil

½ litre milk or, soda water

1 tsp. vanilla essence

8-10tblap. Heaped flour

A little salt

1-2 tsp. sugar

Extra oil and powdered sugar

Method

Mix all the above except the extra oil and sugar. The batter should not be too thick or too thin. Grease a griddle or non-stick pan after heating. Use a small round spoon (e.g. soup spoon) to take batter and place on greased griddle or non-stick pan   Place 4-5 spoons of batter in each batch depending on the size of the pan. When bubbles begin to appear turn over carefully with a spatula and cook the reverse side. Brush pan with oil using the back of a teaspoon after every alternate batch of pancakes. Keep pancakes warm in a food flask covered with a tea towel. When all ready, turn out in a flat dish and sprinkle with powdered or icing sugar. Can also serve the pancakes with any jam sauce or liquid molasses (Bengali '*Nalen Gur*'), maple syrup, honey, cream, or a dollop of beaten cottage or cream cheese.

Jam Sauce:

In a small saucepan put 2 heaped tblsp. any jam and 1 cup water. Bring to boil, lower heat, and simmer a couple of minutes. Serve with pancakes separately in a sauce boat.

COTTAGE CHEESE PANCAKES

4 oz. cottage cheese	4 oz. plain unsweetened yogurt strained
4 oz. castor or fine sugar	2 eggs
1 tsp. vanilla essence	4 oz. (or a little more) flour sifted

Method

Mix cottage cheese, yogurt and sugar and beat well. Add the eggs one at a time and keep beating after each addition till well blended. Add the vanilla essence. Fold in enough flour to get a dropping consistency. Drop the batter in rounds with a soup- spoon on a non-stick fry pan or griddle. When bubbles begin to appear on the surface turn with a spatula and cook the other side for a few seconds till ready. To test, insert a toothpick in the centre of the pancake. If it comes out dry it should be done. Serve the pancakes hot sprinkled with sugar or spread with marmalade, lemon curd, butter flavoured with orange juice and rind, brandy butter or any other jam/jelly or flavouring of choice.

CHOCOLATE PANCAKE DESSERT

10-12 (more or less) thin pancakes or crepes

1 tblsp. grated chocolate

2 cups (more or less) thick chocolate custard and pudding

1 tblsp. grated almonds

Method

Butter the bottom and sides of a round (8" to 10") oven proof dish. Place one pancake at the base and spread generously with the custard. Alternate, with pancake and custard up to 1" from the top of the dish. End with a pancake tucking the sides in slightly so they don't curl up. Sprinkle top with grated chocolate and almond. Bake in a low oven for about 15–20 minutes. Cool and serve cut in slices with fresh cream if desired

Variation:

In place of chocolate custard/pudding any other flavoured custard/pudding may be used. e.g. orange, lemon, strawberry, coffee etc. Garnish top appropriately e.g. orange/lemon rind, chopped strawberries, almond etc. etc.

DALIA OR BORGUL MALPUA (CRACKED WHEAT PANCAKES)

1 cup fine *dalia*

¼ cup or less milk

2 tblsp. sugar (more or less)

2-4 tblsp. oil for frying

¼ cup thickened (almost solid) milk

¼ tsp. aniseed or, cinnamon powder

1 tsp. raisin

Method

Soak *dalia* for about 1 hr or more. Mix with the thickened milk and enough fresh milk to form a thick batter. Stir in all the other ingredients. The mixture should not be too thin or too thick. Brush a non-stick pan with oil and heat slightly. Drop batter by the teaspoon and spread as much as possible with the back of a flat spoon. If necessary, dribble a little more oil from the sides. When bubbles appear turn over and let the other side brown. Drain on paper towels and serve. More than one at a time can be fried depending on the size of the fry pan. This can be served with tea or coffee or as a dessert with cream.

Variation:

1. The thickened milk may be omitted and replaced with only fresh milk according to the amount required to get the correct batter consistency.
2. 2-4 tblsp. condensed milk can be used instead of thickened milk and sugar.
3. Omit the sugar. Make a sugar syrup with 1 cup sugar and 2 cups water. Keep warm. After draining the malpuas dip them in the syrup for a couple of minutes.

CZECH APPLE STRŰDEL

Dough:

1 tblsp. white vinegar	1 egg
A pinch of salt	1 cup tepid water
650 gm. flour	

Filling:

2-4 tblsp. breadcrumbs or, desiccated coconut	1 kg. apple grated
1-2 tblsp. lemon juice	½ tsp. ground cinnamon
1-2 tblsp. butter	1 tblsp. lemon rind grated
125 gm. sugar or to taste	Icing sugar

Method

Put vinegar, egg, salt in the water in a blender and blend. Now add the flour all at once mix and knead well to a soft dough. Cover with a tea towel or cheese cloth and let it rest for ½ hour. Roll out on a floured board wafer thin. Sprinkle dough with either breadcrumbs or coconut so that the filling does not stick to the dough. Mix the apple with the sugar, cinnamon, lemon juice and rind. Spread filling evenly over the breadcrumbs. Once more sprinkle breadcrumbs/coconut lightly over the filling. Dot with the butter. Gently roll up the dough with the filling to resemble a large flat sausage. Carefully lift strüdel on to a greased and floured baking tray and bake in a moderately hot oven for 20-30 minutes or till done. While still warm cut in slices, sprinkle with icing sugar and serve. The strüdel should be crisp and soft but not hard.

FRUIT WAFFLES/FRITTERS/PANCAKES

(Mix any puréed fruit e.g. papaya, mango, apple, pineapple etc. to the waffle/fritter/pancake batter and proceed cooking the usual way. This is convenient if fruit is over ripe and not so tasty eaten fresh.)

1 cup flour	1 tsp. baking powder
A pinch of salt	1-2 tblsp. sugar
1-2 eggs	Milk

Method

Mix all the dry ingredients. Add the eggs one at a time and stir to mix. Next add enough milk to form a thick batter of pouring consistency. Grease a griddle lightly with butter or oil and drop a teaspoonful of batter turning when one side is ready. For the pancake use a teaspoon of batter and spread with the back of the spoon as thin as possible. Waffles have to be made in a waffle maker.

Note:

Fruits can be chopped small instead of puréed.

DÁRAZSFESZEK – (HUNGARIAN SWEET PASTRY)

1 oz. dry yeast

7½ oz. sugar

3 egg yolks

A pinch salt

6 liquid oz. milk (approx.)

2½ oz. butter or margarine

500 gm. flour sieve

Method

Cream yeast with a little warm milk and a little sugar to a smooth paste and leave for 10 minutes till bubbles start to form. Now mix all the other ingredients and the yeast with a wooden spoon in a beating motion (not stirring). Alternately mix and beat in a food processor. Cover and put aside for 2 hours until the dough rises to double. Divide into 2 balls and roll out flat, about 1cm. Brush with oil. Sprinkle with roasted ground pea nuts or cinnamon sugar or chocolate, raisins etc. Top with castor sugar to taste and finally a sprinkle of scant salt. Roll up dough like Swiss roll and cut in slices. Grease a flat baking sheet and sides of cake with oil. Bake in a moderate oven for about 20 minutes. This is good eaten while still fresh and warm. It does not taste so good after 2 days. However, as an extreme measure reheat slightly in the microwave and serve immediately.

LANGOSH

1½ tblsp. dry yeast	1 tsp. sugar
½ litre tepid milk	20 oz. flour
A pinch salt	4 tblsp. oil

Grated or powdered garlic, chilli powder or plain salt for sprinkling

Method

Cream yeast, sugar and 2-3 tblsp milk to a paste. Keep aside till bubbles begin to form. Add the flour sifted with salt, and rest of the milk and mix the dough should be soft. If necessary, add more milk or water. Knead well. While kneading smear a little oil in the palms of the hand so that the dough does not stick to the hands or dish. Cover and keep in a warm place (not hot). Let rise till double. Roll 1½" thick. Now slice in rounds. Pull and stretch with hands as much as possible without tearing dough. The centre of the langosh should be thin and the edges a little thicker. Deep fry. Sprinkle with any of the above options. Serve hot. A good tea-time or with drinks snack.

CHEESECAKE

Pastry:

2 tblsp. sugar	1 tblsp. butter (preferable) or, margarine
1 egg	½ tsp. vanilla essence
2 tblsp. flour	½ tsp. baking powder

Filling:

½ cup milk (more or less)	1 lb. ricotta cheese
2 eggs	1 tblsp. butter
8 oz. sugar	1 tsp. lemon rind grated
3 tblsp. flour	1 tblsp. raisins

Method

Cream the sugar and butter till well mixed. Add the egg, vanilla essence and once again mix well. Sift the flour and baking powder. Add to the creamed mixture. Line a pie pan evenly with the mixture.

Add enough milk to the cheese to get a porridge like consistency. Next add the eggs followed by the rest of the ingredients except the raisins. These should be added at the last moment or else they will sink to the bottom. Mix well till there are no lumps remaining. Fill the pastry case with the mixture. Bake in a slow oven for approx. 1 hour. Cool, cut in slices and serve.

BASIC SCONES

1 lb. flour

¼ tsp. salt

3 oz. butter

6 tsp. level baking powder

2 tblsp. (or more) fine sugar

½-¾ pt. milk/ sour milk/ yogurt

2 tblsp. heaped currants/ sultanas/ raisins/ peels, or half and half, if any

Method

Sift flour, baking powder, salt, and sugar all together. Rub the butter into the dry ingredients. Add milk or substitute a little at a time to form the dough which should not be dry but soft and pliable. Now add the fruit used and mix well. Place dough on a floured board and roll to about ½" thickness. Cut in rounds, the size of a medium jam jar lid, and place on a buttered baking sheet or tray. Brush tops of scones with milk. Bake in a hot oven for about 15-25 minutes or till done. While still warm split the scones in half and sandwich with butter/jam/jelly/sweetened cream/cottage/ricotta cheese etc. This quantity should make about 24 scones.

CHEESE SCONES

8 oz. flour sieved

3 tsp. level baking powder

4 oz. grated cheese

A pinch of salt

2 oz. butter

Cold milk as required for mixing

Method

Sift and mix the flour, salt, and baking powder in a bowl. Add the butter and then the cheese. Mix all preferably by hand. Add enough milk gradually to make a soft but not a sticky dough. Form into a ball. Do not knead much. Put the dough on a floured board. Pat dough with the rolling pin first and then roll about ½" or a little more thick. Cut in rounds with a pastry cutter. Should make 8-10 scones. Put the scones on a greased baking tray. Brush the tops with milk. Bake in a hot oven in the middle shelf for about 15-20 minutes. When ready, cool, split and sandwich with butter. Serve immediately. This makes a good tea-time snack but is equally interesting served for lunch or dinner in place of bread rolls.

GUYANESE RICH COCONUT BENS

8 oz. butter margarine

8 oz. castor sugar

3 eggs

1 tsp. vanilla essence

1-2 tsp. rum (optional)

8 oz. flour

1 level tsp. baking powder

¼ tsp. salt

½ a large coconut grated or, 1-1½ cup desiccated coconut

Method

Beat butter and sugar together till creamy. Beat in one egg at a time. Add the vanilla and rum, if using, with the last egg and mix all till well blended. Sift flour and baking powder and salt together. Add this to the butter mixture. Next add the coconut. Mix all well to a soft dripping consistency. Grease patty pans and lightly dust with flour. ¾ fill the pans with the batter. Bake in a hot oven. Cool on wire tray and gently ease bens out of the pans. Dust tops with icing sugar if desired.

TEATIME AND COCKTAIL SNACKS

CHEESE SNACKS

200 gm. flour

100 gm. cheese grated

½ tsp. pepper

2 eggs separated

1 tblsp. caraway seeds for sprinkling

1 tsp. heaped baking powder

½ tsp. salt

150 gm. butter or margarine

A little milk or fresh cream

Method

Mix all the dry ingredients except caraway seeds. Add softened butter or margarine and egg yolks. Mix all well with a wooden spoon. Last of all use enough milk or fresh cream to bind the dough. Use hands to mix if necessary but do not knead. Roll out ¼" thick and cut into cheese straw shapes or any other shape of your choice. Brush top with egg white lightly and sprinkle caraway seeds on top. Bake in a moderate oven for 10-15 minutes or till golden. A good snack for munching with drinks.

CHEESE PAKORAS

I prefer a strong flavoured cheese – the stronger the better – for this recipe. However, those who are averse to very strong cheese may use a milder cheese of choice. Cottage cheese can be substituted for strong cheese.

4 tblsp. flour	1 tsp. baking powder
½-1 tsp. freshly ground black pepper	4 tblsp. cheese grated or powdered
1 tsp. salt – less if cheese is salty	½ tsp. red chilli powder, paprika or cayenne (optional)
6-8 tblsp. full-cream milk	½ cup oil for frying
2 eggs	

Method

In a bowl mix the first six ingredients. Add the eggs and enough milk to make a smooth and soft dough. Heat oil in a deep pan or a small wok and drop the dough in it in teaspoonfuls. When the pakoras are golden brown remove from wok, drain on paper towels, and serve hot with any favourite chutney, pickle, sauce, or dip. If the oil gets too hot reduce the heat or the pakoras will get burnt. This is a quick snack to make for unexpected guests.

Variation:

If preferred, the above can also be made in the oven instead of deep frying. In this case, before adding the egg and milk add 1 tblsp melted butter or oil to the sifted ingredients. Omit the rest of the oil. Make the dough a little more stiff by using less milk or the pakoras will spread flat while baking. Now drop by teaspoonfuls on a greased and floured baking tray leaving enough gaps between each pakora. Bake in a moderate oven for 5-10 minutes. Cool on a wire tray and serve as above.

CHEESE BALLS

1 cup cheese (preferably cheddar or any cooking cheese grated	2 tblsp. flour
1 tsp. (heaped) baking powder	1 tsp. or less garlic powder (optional)
1 tsp. paprika	1 small onion grated (optional)
2 tsp. melted butter/oil	2 tblsp. (more or less) milk
Extra oil for frying	Salt and pepper to taste

Method

Mix all the dry ingredients together. Add the butter/oil and stir lightly. Next add enough milk stirring to get a thick batter consistency. Deep or shallow fry by dropping batter in small spoonfuls in the oil. Alternately this can also be cooked in a hot oven. Grease and flour a baking sheet and drop batter in small spoonfuls keeping enough space in between each for the balls to spread. Serve hot.

Variation:

1. The above mixture can be spread thickly on bread halves or squares with the crusts trimmed and then either baked or fried. They can also be put under the broiler in which case medium toast the bread
2. The above mixture can also be spread on bread slices with the crusts trimmed and then rolled and fried or baked in a hot oven till done – about 3-5 minutes. These can also be either deep or shallow fried in oil.
3. 1-2 tblsp finely chopped spring onions can be used in place of onion. 1 tblsp. finely chopped green pepper ca also be used if so desired.

SAGO BHUJIA

1 cup sago ground

¼ cup desiccated or, fresh grated coconut

Salt and chilli powder to taste

½ tsp. whole cumin

1-1½ cup water

2 tblsp. ground peanuts

1 tblsp. oil

3-4 curry leaves

A little desiccated or freshly grated coconut and a few freshly chopped coriander leaves for garnishing

Method

Soak sago in water for 5-10 minutes if fine and ½ hour if course. Strain the water and throw it away Mix sago with coconut, peanuts, salt, and chilli powder. Heat oil. Put in the cumin. When it splutters add the curry leaves. Add the sago mixture and fry a light beige colour. Serve sprinkled with coconut and coriander leaves.

Variations:

1 medium potato cut in small cubes and 2 tblsp peas may be added. Either pre-boil the potatoes and add with the peas and sago or fry the potatoes a light golden and then add together with the peas and sago.

This is a delicious tea-time snack.

JAPANESE BEANS ROLLED IN PORK

10-12 French green beans

10-12 pork slices

1 tblsp. red or white wine

Salt to taste

1 tblsp. soy sauce

Oil for frying

Method

Remove strings and nip the edges of the beans. Half boil in salted water or steam. Marinate pork slices in soy sauce and wine for about ½ hour. Rest 2-3 slices of pork on a board and pound a little with the back of a knife or meat tenderizer. Place 2-3 long beans on top and roll the meat around covering the beans. A little bit of the beans should stick out from both ends of the roll. Shallow fry on low to medium heat till done. Serve as a snack.

METHI (FENUGREEK) STRAWS

This is basically a tea-time savoury snack which is a change from the usual sandwich. It may also be served with mid-morning coffee, or with drinks.

1 cup flour	Salt and black pepper to taste
¼ tsp. chilli powder (optional)	1 tsp. whole cumin seeds
1 tsp. finely ground fenugreek seeds	or 2 tblsp. finely chopped fresh fenugreek leaves
Water for making dough	2 tblsp. fat (ghee, butter, margarine or even oil)

Method

Mix all the above ingredients. Add water to make a stiff dough. Roll out dough to ¼" thickness and cut into strips like cheese straws. The dough may also be cut with a cookie cutter to resemble small biscuits. These can be deep or shallow fried or baked in a medium hot oven till golden. These taste better baked which can be stored in a tight fitting jar for about a fortnight.

POTATO CRISPS

250 gm. flour

2 tsp. level baking powder

Salt and pepper to taste

1 tsp. paprika or to taste (optional)

250 gm. potatoes boiled and mashed

250 gm. butter or margarine

1 egg

Method

Sift the flour with the baking powder, salt, pepper and paprika if using. Next add the potato and butter/margarine. Blend all well. Last of all add the egg to bind. Roll out on a floured board about 1/8" thick. With a knife make a crisscross pattern on top without cutting right through. Now cut out small rounds with a biscuit cutter – approximately 1" in diameter. Line a baking sheet with grease proof paper. Brush with oil lightly and then sprinkle flour on top. Place crisps gently on the sheet and bake in a moderate oven till golden brown – 5-10 minutes. A little more time may be needed depending on individual ovens.

PRESERVED POTATOES CHIPS

4-5 large potatoes

1 tblsp. salt or to taste

4 pts. water

1 tsp. chilli powder or to taste (optional)

Method

Scrub potatoes under cold running water well. The peel may be left on or off. Slice wafer thin in the food processor or with a manual slicing gadget. Bring water to boil. Add salt. When water begins to boil add the potato slices. Cook till the wafers become transparent (starchy coloured) and are only half cooked. Drain and pat dry with paper or a tea towel. Coat with the chilli powder if using. Spread out on a tray lined with paper and further dry in the sun or in the oven at the lowest temperature. Store in a jar with a tight lid. Keeps for about 1 year. When required take out and quickly deep fry.

CHUCHURBAWANG

(The real meaning of Chuchurbawang is fried onions in Indonesian. However, it is basically a batter fried pancake or fritter of seasonal mixed vegetables.)

1-2 cups mixed vegetables shredded fine – spinach, cabbage, large onions, spring onions, celery leaves and stems

4-6 oz, flour

1-2 eggs

Salt to taste

½ cup water (approx.)

Method

Put the vegetables in a bowl. Add enough flour to vegetables for pancakes. Add the eggs and mix all. Now add the salt and enough water to form dropping consistency. Dip a rounded spoon in oil. Place batter on the oiled spoon and then deep fry. Serve immediately with soya and chilli sauce as a snack or as an accompaniment to any other dish.

Variations:

Shrimps, shredded or minced chicken, beef, pork or lamb may also be used. If using meat cook a little before adding to the vegetables. Shredded carrots may also be added.

SURPRISE POTATOES

3 cups boiled and mashed potatoes – may be done the day before and kept in the refrigerator

2 tsp. corn flour/cornstarch or, potato flour

1 tsp. plain white flour

1 tsp. salt to taste

2-3 tblsp. oil or as required

½ cup more or less breadcrumbs

1 egg

Chutney Filling

2 tblsp. coconut finely grated

½ cup water

1-2 tblsp. cold milk

1 onion minced

1½" piece ginger minced

1 large clove garlic minced

½ tsp. cumin powder

1 green chilli chopped

½-1 tsp. salt or, to taste

2-3 fresh mint leaves

2 tsp. parsley finely chopped

1 tsp. sugar

1 tsp. lemon juice

Method

For the filling - In a saucepan soak coconut in the water and milk for about 1 hr. Next heat it and let it come to the boil. Lower heat and simmer for 10–15 minutes or longer – approximately ½ hr. This helps to bring out the flavour of the milk. Remove from heat and cool. Add all the other ingredients. Purée in a blender or food processor. Keep aside till required.

Mix potatoes, corn starch, flour, salt, and egg. Make small balls the size of a table tennis ball. Make a hollow in the centre of each ball and put a little filling. Cover the hollow and roll smooth. Roll the balls in breadcrumbs and keep aside for ½ hour. Shallow fry in hot oil.

Variations:

The filling can be varied according to the individual's taste. Egg, vegetable, fish, or meat may be used as filling, cooked with different spices – just let the imagination go wild!! However, as these are eaten as snacks the filling should not be too bold. It is advisable to put the mixture in the blender or food-processor, to get a purée like texture.

BHAKARI VADI

2 cups boiled and mashed potatoes

1-2 tblsp. lime juice

1-2 tblsp. fresh coriander or parsley leaves chopped

1½ tsp. sugar

1 cup flour

3 tsp. chickpea flour (*besan*) or cornflour

Salt to taste

1/3 tsp. each of ground green chilli, ginger, and garlic

1 cup oil

Water as required

Method

Mix potatoes, chickpea flour, juice salt, sugar, spices, and coriander leaves. Keep aside.

Rub 1 tsp oil into the flour. Add enough water to make a dough of rolling consistency. Divide dough into small portions. On a floured board roll each portion ¼" thick into long strips. Spread a layer of potato mixture on the dough. Roll up dough and cut in ½ "slices. Deep fry in oil.

PLACKY or CZECH SAVORY POTATO PANCAKES

1 egg

2 medium onions

3-5 tblsp. flour

Salt and black pepper to taste

Water for dough only if necessary

5 medium potatoes grated fine

4 tblsp. oil or, as required

2-4 cloves garlic minced finely

½-1 tsp. marjoram

Method

Add the egg to the potato and mix well. Chop 1 onion finely and fry lightly till golden in 1 tsp oil. Grate the second onion and add to the potato. (The potato and onion may be grated together.) Add the fried onion and all the rest of the ingredients with enough flour to the potato to make a soft pliable dough. Warm oil just enough to cover the bottom of a fry pan and shallow fry large spoonfuls of dough like fritters or thick pancakes. A nonstick fry pan will consume less oil. If mixture gets too thick add a little water.

CLAM CANAPÉS

250 gm. cream cheese	200 gm. canned clams
½ tsp. garlic salt	1 tsp. Worcestershire sauce
Salt and pepper or, paprika to taste	1 tblsp. finely chopped parsley

Method

Soften cheese with 1-2 tblsp. clam juice. Add all the other ingredients and mix till smooth. Spread on round salted biscuits or squares/rounds of buttered toasts or on water biscuits. Garnish with a sprinkling of chopped parsley.

Clams may be substituted with 200 gm. canned crab meat. Proceed as above.

CLAM DIP

6-8 oz. sour cream

½ tsp. cayenne (optional)

2-3 (depending on the number of guests) artichokes cooked

1 small can or, 1 cup clam minced

1 tsp. paprika

Method

Add the sour cream to the minced clams and stir till all well blended. Add the cayenne if using. Place dip in a bowl and sprinkle top with the paprika. Place bowl in the centre of a flat platter and surround with artichokes. Break the leaves and dip into the bowl before eating.

OLIVE and BACON CANAPÉS

12 (more or less depending on the number of guests) green/black olives

6 slices of bacon slightly cooked and cut in half

Method

Wrap each olive with half a slice of bacon. Grill till done. Stick a toothpick on each and serve while hot.

COCKTAIL TID BITS

Several cocktail salted biscuits or, water biscuits or, crisp fried or toasted bread squares

Method

Spread the above biscuits or bread squares with any of the following combinations and garnish with chopped parsley/sweet bel pepper/mint leaves/coriander leaves

1. ¼ cup cream cheese mixed with ¼ tsp or more garlic powder or 1-2 cloves garlic minced very fine.
2. ¼ cup cream or cottage cheese mixed with 1-2 strands of spring onions chopped very fine and garnish with a thin sprinkle of the leaves.
3. ¼ cup cream cheese mixed with either ¼ chopped tomato, or yellow/red/green bel pepper of choice and garnished with the same.
4. ¼ cup cream cheese mixed with ½ tsp chopped any fresh herb or ¼ tsp any dried herb and garnished with the same.

STUFFED DILL PICKLE

If dill is not readily available substitute with either pickled small cucumbers or medium pickled gherkins.

Method

Carefully slice the top and bottom of the dill and then core. Stuff the inside with processed cheese. Cut in slices and stick toothpicks on each and serve.

APPLE and ROQUEFORT CHEESE

1-2 tblsp. mayonnaise

2 tsp. (more or less) lemon juice

2-3 small apples sliced with skin on

1-2 tsp. paprika

¼-½ cup sour cream

1-2 tblsp. (according to taste) roquefort cheese

Chopped parsley for garnish

Method

Mix the mayonnaise, sour cream, lemon juice and cheese. Spread on the apple slices. Sprinkle with paprika and garnish with parsley before serving.

ANCHOVY PUFF

½ cup butter

1 cup flour sifted

3 oz. cream cheese

1-2 tblsp. anchovy paste or as required

Method

Mix butter and cream cheese together. Add the flour and mix till all well blended. Refrigerate for 1 hour or till dough gets hard enough for rolling and not sticky. Sprinkle a board lightly with flour and roll out dough very thin. Cut with a round biscuit cutter 2" across. Spread each round lightly with anchovy paste. Fold over in half. Bake in a moderately hot oven for about 10 minutes. Serve with drinks or at tea-time. These puffs can be kept in the refrigerator all ready and popped into the oven for baking just before serving. Just the dough without the spread can be refrigerated for 4-5 days and taken out when required.

Variation:

The anchovy paste can be substituted with the following – shrimp, fish, chicken, pork liver pastes. Fish sauce, ketchup or any other tangy sauce can be used to the above items as appropriate, to enhance the flavour. Mashed sardines in oil, mustard, or tomato sauce can also be used. For subtle flavoured puffs use just a hint of any of the spreads.

LIVER PATÉ

1 tblsp. oil

1 kg. liver cut small

2 hard-boiled eggs chopped

Salt and pepper to taste

3 medium onions minced

10 tblsp. level butter

½-1 tsp. curry powder

Method

Heat oil. Fry onions till golden. Add liver and fry well. Lower heat, cook covered for another 10 minutes. Take off heat and cool. Put cooled mixture through a mincer or in the food processor. Add the rest of the ingredients and mix well. Put into the food processor a second time. Put in any sized container to shape. Turn out onto a grease proof paper and wrap pate to cover all sides well like a package. Either wrap this package again in aluminium foil or put in a container and refrigerate. Keeps for about 3-4 days. Does not freeze well – might crumble. Spread on plain bread or toast, salted biscuits, crackers etc.

LIVER and PORK PATÉ

750 gm. pork or veal liver	500 gm. bacon
150 gm. fatty pork	1 kg. red onions
4-6 tblsp. parsley chopped	350gm. lean pork
1-2 bay leaves	3-4 eggs
1-2 tsp. garlic powder	1 tsp. thyme chopped
Salt to taste	1 tsp. basil chopped
Lots of fresh ground black pepper	

Method

Grind the liver, bacon, fatty pork, onions, and parsley in a food processor. Dice the lean pork and add to the ground meats etc. along with all the rest of the ingredients. Mix with a thick white sauce as under. Put in 2 loaf tins and bake in a med oven for about 1½ hours or a little longer. Check with a skewer or toothpick which should come out clean when pierced in the centre. Cut in slices and then halve or quarter each slice. Serve chilled. This can be wrapped in foil and frozen for 2-3 months.

White Sauce

4 tblsp. butter	4 tblsp. flour
2 cups undiluted full cream milk powder	Salt and pepper to taste

Make a roux with the above ingredients in a heavy-bottomed saucepan on very low heat. Mix this to the pâté as per directions.

FALAFEL

2 cups chickpeas

2 tblsp. parsley chopped

1 tsp. salt

½ tsp. paprika

Oil for frying

3 cloves garlic

½ tsp. cumin powder

½ tsp. black pepper

½ cup water

Method

Soak chickpeas overnight. Next day grind or put in the food processor with garlic and parsley. Add seasonings and rest of the spices, and enough water to make a smooth paste of dropping consistency. Fry in hot oil in small round balls. Serve with *tahina* Sauce. Makes an excellent cocktail snack.

Tahina Sauce

¾ cup tahina (ground white sesame seeds)

4-6 oz. fresh lemon juice

2 tsp. fresh mint leaves finely chopped

½ tsp. cumin powder

10-12 cloves garlic minced

2 tsp. parsley finely chopped

1 tsp soya sauce

Salt and black pepper

½ cup water or less according to the lemon juice used. If too sour add a little sugar

Method

Place tahina in a blender. Alternately, add water and lemon juice to it. Now add all the other ingredients. Blend all well. Serve with Falafel.

Variations: <u>For Serving</u> –

1. The sauce may be added to boiled and mashed yolks of egg and then put back into the white casing and served for cocktails
2. Can be used as a dressing for salads.

3. Roast eggplants in the oven, grill or top of the stove. Peel burnt skin and then mash the pulp. Mix the pulp with tahina and serve as an accompaniment with meat or fish.
4. Tahina may also be served as a dip for cucumber, carrot etc. stick and tomato segments.

DALIA PAKORA (CRACKED WHEAT or BORGUL BALLS)

1 cup *dalia*

2 tblsp. fresh coriander leaves chopped fine

Salt to taste

1 large onion chopped

1-2 green chillis minced (optional)

Oil for frying

Method

Soak *dalia* in just enough water to cover for 1-2 hours or more. Strain and squeeze out water by pressing down with the palm. Mix with the rest of the ingredients. (½ tsp. paprika can be used in place of green chillis.) Heat oil and deep fry pakoras in tea spoonfuls. Take out with a slotted spoon and drain on paper towels. Serve with any green or coconut chutney. The pakoras can be shallow fried in a nonstick pan. The deep fried pakoras are always tastier!

RICE CAKES or PAKORAS

1-2 cups (more or less) left over soggy rice	1-2 onion slices crisply fried
1-2 green chillis deseeded and chopped	4-5 spring onions chopped fine
½ bunch fresh coriander leaves chopped	Salt to taste
1-2 tblsp. ketchup, *achar* or any other sauce	½-1 cup oil for frying
4-6 tblsp. flour	2-3 chopped bacon fried crisp

Method

Mix all the ingredients except flour and oil to the rice. Form into small balls the size of golf balls or flatten into cakes or hamburger shapes. Roll in dry flour to coat all over. Heat oil and either deep fry or shallow fry. Place on paper towels to drain oil and serve with any sauce, pickle, chutney etc. with drinks or tea/coffee.

KATJANG MANA LAGI (INDONESIAN PEANUT BRITTLE)

1 kg. grilled or roasted peanuts without any butter or oil

½ cup more or less oil

Batter

1 egg	1 tblsp. salt or, to taste
3 tblsp. sugar	1 tsp. garlic paste
½ cup milk	½ cup water
1 cup flour sifted	Oil for frying

Method

Mix the above batter ingredients well. Drop the peanuts into the batter and mix to coat. Heat oil in a small wok and fry in spoonfuls little at a time. Drain on paper towel and either serve immediately or store in a tight-fitting lid. Keeps for 2-3 weeks.

REMPEJEK* (INDONESIAN PEANUT CHIPS)

* Pronounced *"Rumpuye"*

500 gm. peanut shelled and cleaned

Sufficient oil for deep frying

Batter:

1 tblsp. salt or to taste

1 tsp. coriander powder

1 tsp. turmeric

1 tblsp. ground almonds (optional)

1 tsp. garlic powder or, according to taste

1 cup flour

½ cup potato flour/corn starch/corn flour

1¼-1½ cups (more or less) coconut milk**

Method

Mix salt, coriander powder, turmeric, almonds, and garlic powder. Next add the flour and potato flour or substitute and stir. Last of all add the coconut milk and keep stirring till all well mixed and smooth with no lumps. Now add the peanuts to this batter and stir to make sure the peanuts are well coated. Heat oil and fry in medium or soup spoonfuls or if preferred teaspoonfuls. Drain chips on paper towel when ready. Store in an airtight jar. Rempejek should keep for 2-3 weeks.

** Readymade coconut milk or coconut powder with instructions, are available in the market. However, if using fresh coconut milk use the following method. 1 ½ cups grated coconut and 1 cup lukewarm water. Cover coconut with a little of the water and let soak for about 10 minutes. Squeeze out all the water and strain. Add a little more water and repeat the process. Continue in this way till all the water is used up. Discard the coconut or keep it aside to use for filling sweets, cakes, or desserts. Use the strained water or coconut milk for the batter

----

LUNCHEON MEAT KOFTAS

1 can luncheon meat

1 medium capsicum de-seeded and chopped fine

1 fresh green chilli chopped fine

1-2 tblsp. flour

1-2 tblsp. tomato ketchup

2 tblsp. heaped corn flour

2-3 spring onions chopped fine

1 tsp. curry powder (optional)

Oil for shallow frying

Method

Break up the luncheon meat and mash lightly with a fork. Add the rest of the ingredients excepting flour and oil. Mix well. Form into small *kofta* balls. Spread flour on a flat plate or dish and roll the koftas in it. Now shallow fry in a non-stick or any other fry pan, which should be brushed lightly with oil. Makes 30-40 koftas.

Serve with the following sauce: In a bowl mix 8 tblsp ketchup, 4 tblsp *kasaundi* or strong mustard. If required add a dash of tabasco or chilli sauce or ½ tsp. paprika.

Variations:

The luncheon meat can be substituted with cooked sausage meat, chopped ham or sardines in oil. In the case of the latter a little extra corn flour may be needed to subdue the oil of the sardines. For this, omit the ketchup.

MINCE KEBABS

500 gm. mince – beef, mutton, chicken, or soya granules	2-3 onions chopped
5-6 cloves garlic chopped	½" piece ginger sliced
4-5 black pepper corns	3-4 cloves
2-3 green cardamoms de-seeded	1" piece cinnamon broken into small pieces
2-3 bay leaves crumbled	Salt to taste
¼ tsp. paprika (optional)	1-2 green chillis deseeded and chopped (optional)
1 cup water	2 tsp. chickpea flour
2 tsp. ketchup	¼-½ cup oil
2-4 tblsp. flour	

Method

Cook all the above ingredients (except chick-pea flour, green chillis, ketchup, oil and flour) with the water until done. Dry off the water, if any. Mixture should be moist and not watery. Put the mixture with the green chillis if using, through a grinder a couple of times or in a food processor till smooth. Add the ketchup to moisten and for extra flavour. Mix with a wooden spoon. Now add the chick-pea flour to bind – making sure it is well blended by kneading well. Form into medium or small round flattened cakes or kebabs. Roll in dry flour and shallow fry brown on a griddle on medium heat. Make sure the insides of the kebabs are done by piercing the centre with a toothpick. Serve hot garnished with thinly sliced onion rings and lime. Thin slices of tomato or/and cucumber can also be served with the kebabs.

Note.

Both the green chillis and the paprika can be used or left out or only one of them may be used. If using soya granules or chunks (*nutrella*), soak in water just to cover for ½ hr and then proceed as above. Green chillis should be added to this along with 1-2 tblsp chopped fresh coriander leaves. This is a good snack for vegetarians.

EGG KEBAB

4-5 hard-boiled eggs mashed	1 very large boiled and mashed potato
2 tsp. fresh lime juice	2 tblsp. finely chopped fresh coriander leaves, or 1 tsp. each of coriander and cumin powder
1 tblsp. flour	Salt and black pepper to taste
4-6 tblsp. water	breadcrumbs
1 tblsp. oil	½ tsp. chilli powder or to taste

Method

Mix egg, potato, lime juice, coriander leaves, or cumin and coriander powder, chilli powder, salt and pepper well. Form into balls the size of a table tennis ball or marble.

Make a smooth batter of the flour and water. Add a little more water if necessary. The batter should be the consistency of a beaten egg – not too thin and not too thick. Dip kebabs in batter and then roll in breadcrumbs. If necessary, repeat the procedure once more and let rest for 5-10 minutes. Brush non-stick pan with oil and fry the kebabs slowly till all sides well browned. Alternately brush kebabs with oil and brown under the grill evenly constantly turning or microwave on a carousel on high for 1 minute or till golden.

Serve with ketchup or mint chutney or a combination of ketchup, *kasaundi* (spicy mustard paste available ready-made in stores) and chilli sauce. The latter is piquantly delicious.

EGYPTIAN KABEBA

Dough:

2 cups '*borghul*' (cracked wheat or '*dālia*') soaked overnight

2 tblsp. flour

Salt to taste

1 tsp. cumin powder

Filling:

500 gm. ground meat (lamb)

Pepper and salt to taste

2 tsp. cumin powder

1 large onion chopped

1 cup or less water

2-4 tblsp. pine nuts browned

Oil for deep frying

Method

Cook all the filling ingredients except the nuts without oil but just enough water to cover. Dry off excess water if any. The filling should be moist.

Mix the dough ingredients. Add a little water to bind the dough. Put in the food processor or pass through a meat grinder. The dough should be smooth. Shape the dough onto small balls the size of a table tennis ball. Flatten centre with thumb and put some filling inside topped with a few pine nuts. Cover, roll and shape into fingers or croquets. Dip palms in water before shaping the 'kabebas'. Deep fry in oil. Drain on paper towel. Serve with assorted pickled vegetables such as cucumber, onions, carrots, radish etc. A good snack with drinks or starter with an assortment of kebabs.

QUICK KEBABS OR KOFTAS

2 medium slices of bread soaked in water	1 kg. ground meat
1 bunch fresh coriander leaves chopped chilli powder or paprika to taste (optional)	1 tsp. each coriander and cumin powder freshly roasted and ground
4 tblsp. (more or less) flour	2 eggs or, 3 yolks slightly beaten
Salt to taste	2 onions finely grated

Method

Squeeze out water from the bread by pressing between the palms. Mix with all the above ingredients, except oil, together thoroughly till smooth. Wet hands and form into small koftas or shape into flattened kebabs. To get uniform shaped kebabs use the lid of any jar the size required. Dip lid in cold water, pack with meat, smoothen with a palette or knife and then turn out on a floured board. Roll koftas/kebabs in dry flour and either deep or shallow fry till cooked through and brown on the outside. Serve as snacks with sliced raw onions, lime, and cucumber.

Note:

Ground beef can be substituted in place of mutton.

MOWCHA or BANANA FLOWER KOFTAS

1 mowcha cleaned, boiled, and mashed	1 tsp. each coriander and cumin powder
2-4 tblsp. oil for frying	1 bunch fresh coriander leaves minced fine
A handful of raisins	4 tblsp. chickpea flour (*besan*)
Salt to taste	Water as required

Method

Fry the *mowcha* with coriander and cumin powder in 1-2 tsp. oil. Take off heat and cool. Form into small *koftas* or balls. Make a depression in the centre with thumb. Fill depression with minced coriander leaves and raisins. Cover the filling and re-form into koftas. Make a thick batter with the *besan*, salt and water. Beat and keep aside for ½ hr. Heat remaining oil, Dip *koftas* in the batter and deep fry. Drain on paper towels. Good with tea, coffee, or drinks.

Variations:

½ cup shrimps or ground meat may be added to the mow-cha. 1 tsp onion, ½ tsp each of garlic and ginger pastes can also be added to the mixture during cooking.

Shrimp or Ground Meat Koftas:

Koftas can also be made as above minus the *mowcha*.

Fillings:

Fillings can also be varied – desiccated or fresh ground coconut and minced green chillis with or without the seeds can be substituted or added with the original filling. Chopped fresh mint leaves also make a good substitute.

The besan batter may be omitted for all the koftas. For a lighter kofta roll them in dry flour and shallow fry.

All the above minus the fillings and the batter make good fillings for *samosas* or patties. In the latter do not make them into balls. Just cook with all the spices mentioned or add some others such as *garam masala*, ketchup etc.

To clean mowcha

Take out the outer red leaves layer by layer. Take out the yellow flowers in between each layer. Discard the stick from the centre of each flower. Chop and boil. It may be easier to clean *mowcha* with a little oil rubbed into the palms of the hands. Actually, it is not as difficult as it seems. Not all *mowchas* are edible. If in doubt, soak the cleaned flowers in hot salted water over night. Next morning discard the water, wash the vegetable several times, and then boil before proceeding with the chosen recipe.

MOWCHA (BANANA FLOWER) KEBABS

(This is ideally made from left over Bengali "*mowcha ghonto*" as under the "Curried Items in this book – easy and quick!)

Put left over "*mowcha ghonto*" in a food processor and process till mushy. Dust palms with dry flour and form small kebabs or *koftas* with the processed *mowcha*. Make a depression in the centre of each kebab and fill with a mixture of grated coconut, raisins and minced fresh coriander leaves. Chopped fresh green chilli may be added if so desired. Cover filling and once again roll in between the palms to form a round small kebab. Roll kebabs in dry flour and shallow fry in oil. Serve as a vegetarian snack with a mint or coriander chutney with cocktails or afternoon tea.

KANCHKALA or GREEN BANANA BURGERS

¼-½ cup oil	6 green bananas peeled, boiled, and mashed
1 tblsp. onion paste	1 tsp. each of coriander and cumin powder
2 tsp. ginger paste	Salt to taste
½ tsp. turmeric powder	1-2 green chillis deseeded and minced (optional), or 1-2 tsp paprika (optional)
1-2 tblsp. unsweetened yogurt	1-2 tblsp. flour

Method

Heat oil and cook mashed bananas with all the spices and salt till there is no raw smell. If using fresh green chillis, keep aside for adding later. Take off heat and add enough yogurt for binding. Add the green chillis also at this time. When mixture is cool form into small flat burghers. Roll in dry flour. Shallow fry in oil. Serve with raw onion, tomato, and cucumber rings.

SAUSAGE ROLLS

1 lb. sausage meat	1-2 onions chopped
1 medium capsicum minced	1 bunch fresh parsley/coriander leaves chopped
1-2 tblsp. Worcester sauce (optional)	1-2 tblsp. ketchup (optional)
2 lbs. short pastry or, as required	1-2 fresh green chillis deseeded and minced (optional)
1-2 eggs or, 1-2 tblsp. corn flour to bind	1-2 tblsp. milk
1-2 spring onions chopped fine	Salt and pepper to taste

Method

Cook the sausage meat with the onions till the latter is soft and the meat done, over medium heat without any oil. Mix with all the other ingredients well. This is the filling for the rolls.

Roll out pastry on a floured board about ¼" thick. Cut in rounds with a biscuit cutter the size of a small to medium '*puri*'. Put filling in the centre. Fold the two sides towards the centre so that the filling does not escape. Now roll the dough with the filling gently like a sausage and seal the edges with a little water. Brush top with egg or milk or a combination of both to glaze. Bake in a hot oven till done. Serve with green tomato or a cucumber salad with a French dressing or a plain vinegar or lemon juice dressing or any other dressing of choice. This can be served as a light supper dish or a snack.

Variations:
1. Instead of shaping them like rolls they can be shaped like dumplings by pulling up all the sides to the centre. Pressing down slightly and sealing with a little water.
2. Instead of sausage meat, whole cocktail sausages or large sausages cut to the required length can be used as filling. In this case the pastry should be shaped into rolls and the sides may be left slightly open. Glaze and bake as above.

3. Bread dough can also be used in place of short pastry. If using the latter, the actual sausage rather than a filling of sausage meat is preferable. Glaze and bake as above.

ROLLS FROM LEFT-OVER MINCE CURRY

(Another appetizing cocktail/teatime snack from left over *'keema'* or *'keema mattar* 'curry (ground meat/ground mince and pea curry).

Method

Sprinkle freshly chopped coriander leaves on left over *keema/keema mattar* curry. Mix gently. Make short crust pastry. Roll in a round. Cut out portions for mini croissants. Place filling in the widest section and roll up like croissants. Place the croissants carefully on a greased and floured baking tray. Brush tops with milk or egg. Bake in a hot oven – 15-20 minutes. Cool when done and serve with any dip or chutney.

SAVOURY ROLLS

100 gm. butter   1 cup flour

½ cup milk   3-4 eggs separated

Method

Melt butter in a saucepan. Add flour and keep stirring on low heat for a couple of minutes or until well blended. Add milk and continue stirring like *bechamel* sauce till well mixed. Take off heat. Add yolks one by one and mix well. The mixture should be smooth with no lumps. Cool. Fold in stiffly beaten egg whites. Spread on a greased Swiss roll baking tray evenly. Bake in a moderately hot oven. When ready take out of oven and turn out on a cheese cloth or tea towel. Quickly roll holding the ends of the cloth. When cool, unroll and put filling. Re-roll, cut in slices and serve with tea or coffee.

Filling:

1. Mix fresh cream and smoked ham, or,
2. Mix cream cheese and smoked ham, or,
3. Substitute any other filling of your choice

COTTAGE CHEESE HAM ROLLS

250 gm. flour

1 tsp. baking powder

250 gm. (more or less) cooked ham chopped small

250 gm. cottage cheese

250 gm. butter

Method

Sift flour and baking powder together. Crumble cottage cheese and butter into the flour and mix all well and form into a large ball. No need to add any water. Refrigerate dough for several hours, preferably overnight. Take out when required and divide into three balls. Place each on a floured board. Tap top with a rolling pin to flatten and then roll out thin into a round. Cut into eight triangles with a sharp knife starting from the centre. Place a little chopped ham in the wider part of the triangle and start rolling towards the narrow end. Make sure the ham is well tucked in and does not spill out. Press the narrow end or tail down to prevent it from opening out. Use a little cold water if necessary. Hold the two ends of the roll and slightly turn them towards you to form a curve. It should resemble a croissant. Brush tops with milk or egg. Arrange on a baking tray with a little gap between each roll and bake in a hot oven.

If the rolls seem a little soft and runny, refrigerate for ½ hr or more before putting them into the oven. The above quantity should make 24 ham rolls. These are good teatime or cocktail snacks and can be frozen wrapped in foil if not immediately required. The rolls may also be frozen without baking well wrapped in foil and then in freezer bags. They can be taken out 15 -30 mins before putting in the oven. If the rolls are to be eaten as a supper snack or light lunch make larger croissants by dividing each round into only four triangles. Then the above quantity should yield 12 ham rolls. Serve with a tomato or green salad.

PIQUANT SAUSAGES

1 cup red wine

2 cups sugar

250-500 gm. uncooked smoked cocktail sausages

Method

Cook wine and sugar together till the latter melts and the mixture is slightly caramelized. Add sausages to the liquid until cooked. Take out of liquid, stick toothpicks on each and serve as a snack while still hot with mustard.

Variation:

Large sausages cut up small can also be used in place of cocktail sausages. These sausages can be served with poached or fried eggs for breakfast or supper. Mashed potatoes and baked beans are good accompaniments.

If smoked sausages are not available, one can use any plain spicy or flavoured sausage. After taking sausages out of the liquid they can be slightly browned in a non-stick pan.

CHICKEN CHAAT

500 gm. cubed boneless chicken	1 tblsp. oil
1 or 2 medium potatoes cubed (optional)	2 tblsp. heaped *chaat masala*
1-2 tsp. red chilli or hot paprika or Kashmir chilli powder or hot paprika	2 tsp. each freshly roasted and powdered cumin and coriander seeds
½ tsp. freshly ground pepper	A pinch of '*amchoor*' (mango powder)
Salt to taste	2 tblsp. fresh lime juice

Method

Heat oil in a wok. Stir fry chicken, potato, and onion altogether till done. Add all the powders except *amchoor*. Mix well. Take off heat. Add *amchoor* and lime juice. Adjust the latter according to taste. Makes a good snack. May also be served as a filling inside rolls or parathas, cut in 3 or 4 pieces with a toothpick stuck on it for easy handling.

Variation

Small cubes of mutton or beef can be used instead of chicken. In case of beef be sure to use meat from the fillet (undercut) and in the case of mutton – portions from the shoulder or belly are advisable.

Whole corn kernels or green peas can also be added to the 'chaat' during the last minute of cooking just before adding the powders.

SAVORY SESAME MACHINE BISCUITS

700 gm. flour

1 tsp. baking powder

Salt and black pepper to taste

A little paprika (optional)

100 gm. (approx.) sesame seeds

200 gm. butter/margarine/ghee

4 eggs

A little milk (only if necessary) for mixing

Method

Sift flour, baking powder, salt, pepper, paprika if used. Add the sesame seeds and mix. Next add the margarine and eggs, and blend with a hand blender or in the food processor. Add just enough milk to make a pliable dough. Leave to rest in the refrigerator for 1-2 hours or overnight. These biscuits are best shaped if you have a biscuit cutter attachment in your kitchen machine. They can also be shaped with a manual cookie cutter. Failing this, roll the dough on a floured board fairly thin and then cut into any shapes. Place on a baking tray and bake in a hot oven for about 10 minutes. These can be stored for 2-3 months in a jar with a tight lid. These savoury biscuits can be served with tea, coffee or even with drinks.

SAVORY PEANUT BISCUITS

8 oz. white or brown (wheat) flour	1 tblsp. salt or to taste
1 tsp. baking powder	½ tsp. paprika (optional)
½ tsp. black pepper freshly ground (optional)	2 oz. margarine or butter
4 oz. peanuts dry roasted and ground	¼ cup (more or less) milk

Method

Sift all the dry ingredients except ground peanuts together. Add the peanuts and mix. Next add the fat and rub into the mixture. Now add sufficient milk a little at a time to make a stiff and pliable dough. It should not be too dry or too sticky. Roll dough to ¼" thickness and then cut in small (or the size desired) rounds. Place on a greased and floured cookie sheet and bake in a moderate oven for about ½ hr to 45 mins or till done. Loosen biscuits while still hot and leave on the tray to cool. Store in a jar with an air-tight lid. These are good for serving at tea-time or with drinks. They can be served plain or spread with any favourite filling, paste or pâté. Alternatively, serve the biscuits separately with any favourite dip.

Variation:

The peanuts can be added without dry roasting. Just shell and grind them. The peanuts can be substituted with 4 tblsp. of peanut butter in which case reduce the quantity of fat by half. If the peanut butter has salt, then reduce the quantity of salt.

SALTY BISCUITS

1 lb. flour	2-3 tsp. salt
¼ tsp. paprika	½ tsp. whole cumin/caraway seeds
½ tsp. or less garlic powder	2-3 oz. cheddar or any other cheese –powdered or grated fine
8 oz. butter/margarine/any other cooking fat or oil	1-2 eggs

Method

Mix all the dry ingredients together. Cut the fat in and mix till resembles breadcrumbs. Last of all add the eggs one a time. Mix all well to get a soft rolling consistency. If mixture too dry add more eggs as required or use a little milk to get a soft but not sticky dough. Roll to a ¼" thick and cut in small rounds or any other shape with a biscuit cutter. Brush top with milk or egg. Place on a greased and floured baking tray and bake in a moderate oven till done or golden for about 20-30 minutes. Serve plain or with a dip or spread e.g. sour cream dip or a cream cheese spread.

SAVOURY BISCUITS

2 cups flour sifted	3 tsp. level baking powder
6 tblsp. margarine	½-1 tsp. black pepper/paprika/fresh or dried herbs of choice (optional)
2/3 cup cold milk	1 tsp. salt

Method

Mix all the dry ingredients in a bowl. Add fresh herbs finely chopped if using. Next add the margarine and mix till the mixture resembles breadcrumbs. Make a depression in the centre and gradually pour in the cold milk. Draw the flour into the milk from all sides slowly and mix to a soft pliable dough. Turn dough onto a floured board and knead well for about 5 minutes. Roll and flatten dough to ¼" thickness and then cut into rounds with a biscuit cutter to the size required. Lift carefully and transfer to a non-greased baking tray and bake in a moderately hot oven for about 10 mins or till cooked to a golden colour.

NB.

1-2 tblsp grated parmesan or any other mildly flavoured cheese can be used with or without the above options.

LAHNMAHAJAN or LEBANESE PIZZA

Dough:

2½ lb. flour	1 tsp. salt
1½ tsp. dried yeast	1 tsp. sugar
1 tblsp. lukewarm water	Water as required
Shortening as required	Margarine as required
Oil as required	

Filling:

1 lb. ground meat (lamb)	1 tblsp. parsley chopped finely
3 big onions chopped finely	1 cup red vinegar
Salt and pepper to taste	1-2 tblsp. tahina sauce
1 doz. (more or less) pine nuts slit in the middle (optional)	

Method

Dough:

Sift flour and salt and make a well in the centre. In the meantime, place the yeast, sugar, and the lukewarm water in a bowl, stir and cover till dissolved. When bubbles start appearing in the yeast mixture pour the whole into the well of the flour. Fill the well by drawing the flour from the sides and mixing all together. Now add enough water gradually to make a soft dough. This is best done by hand. Form the whole into a ball. Let it rest covered for about 15 minutes – the dough does not have to rise. Divide dough and make into two long sausages for easy handling. In a fry pan melt equal amounts of shortening and margarine – take off heat. Mix with an equal amount of oil. Tear off bits of dough the size of *puris*. Dip in the oil mixture thoroughly and place on a flat dish or table. Spread well by pulling and stretching the sides as much as possible. Now hold one side and lift like a rope and shape by turning into a wheel. Again, it should be the size of a puri but resembling a wheel. Place wheels on a well-greased baking tray. Tuck the end of each wheel into the centre. It does not matter if dough breaks in parts slightly, while pulling and stretching.

***Filling*:**

Mix the lamb, parsley and onions together and then soak in the vinegar for approx. 1 hr. Add salt, pepper and tahina and mix all well together. Put 1 tsp full (or a little more) of the meat mixture on each of the wheels spreading it slightly with the back of the spoon to cover the surface. If desired stick half a pine nut on top of the pizzas. Bake in a moderate oven for about 10 minutes or till light brown. Makes over 2 doz. miniature pizzas.

LAHMEDJUN (ARMENIAN PIZZAS)

1 kg. ground very fatty lamb	1-2 oz. butter (or more if lamb is not fatty)
5-6 tblsp. onion chopped	Salt to taste
1 tsp. allspice powder	A pinch cinnamon powder
A small pinch clove powder	2 tsp. chilli powder or, paprika
¼ tsp. black pepper ground fresh	1 tsp. garlic paste or, grated fine
3 tblsp. parsley chopped	2 tsp. fresh mint chopped
1 tsp. green chilli de-seeded and chopped	500 gm. tomato chopped
1 kg. bread or, pizza dough	

Method

Place meat (add a little butter if meat is less fatty) in a saucepan over moderate heat with the onion. Cook for a few minutes to melt the fat. Add salt and keep mashing constantly with the back of a wooden spoon. Take off heat. Add all the rest of the ingredients except the dough and mix well.

Tear off dough into several small balls the size of golf balls. Sprinkle dry flour on each ball and roll to a round of about 6" across like a small 'chapati'. Grease a baking tray or sheet and place the pizzas on its side by side. Brush tops of each pizza with cold water. Spread the meat mixture on top and bake in a hot oven for about 20 minutes. Serve hot as a teatime, supper, or cocktail snack.

Note.

Beef or veal can be substituted in place of lamb, but it must be very fatty.

CRUMB-FRIED or BATTER-FRIED ROE

500 gm. fresh roe

Salt to taste

1 tblsp. lemon juice or vinegar

½-1 cup oil for deep frying

Method

Coat roe with lemon juice and salt. Place in a covered container and pressure cook for about 5 minutes. Cool, and drain all water. Cut in slices and either deep fry coated with breadcrumbs or in batter. Drain on paper towels and serve hot with tea/coffee or drinks with any sauce, dip, pickle, or chutney of choice.

For Crumb Frying:

Roll roe slices in dry flour and rest for a few minutes. Lightly beat 2 eggs mixed with 2 tblsp. water or milk. Dip roe slices in the egg mixture and roll in breadcrumbs to coat all sides. Repeat twice. Shake off any excess crumbs and let rest for 5-10 minutes. Deep fry over medium heat.

Note. The egg may be substituted with a paste of flour and water which should be the same consistency as egg.

For Batter Frying:

Sift 8 oz. flour with 2 tsp. heaped baking powder. Add 1-2 eggs (optional) and mix well. Next add just enough water or milk or ½ milk and ½ water or only soda water to get a good fritter batter consistency. The batter should not be too thick or too thin. Just right to coat the roe slices evenly. Heat oil and deep fry. If the oil gets too hot reduce heat and again increase, when necessary, i.e. if the oil gets to just warm.

Note: Left-over beer is also a good option for the batter in place of milk, water, or plain soda water.

FISH WAFERS

2-4 tblsp. (more or less) potato or corn flour

¼-½ tsp. paprika or any other seasoning of choice

3 eggs or more

¼-½ tsp. bicarbonate of soda

Salt and pepper to taste

400-450 gm. white boneless fish chopped

1 cup or more oil for deep frying

Method

Sift all the dry ingredients together. Put the raw fish with all the other ingredients except the oil in a blender or food processor. Make sure all the ingredients are mixed well. Cut mixture into wormlike shapes. Heat oil and deep fry crisp. Drain on paper towels. These wafers can be stored in a tight-fitting jar.

PRAWN SNACKS

Method

Marinate medium sized prawns and large thick slices of onions in oil, lemon juice, red wine oregano/Italian herbs for a couple of hours. Cook under the grill or in a non-stick pan turning frequently to cook evenly. Skewer the prawns and onions alternately in toothpicks and serve with cocktails. Serve with a sour cream or hot tomato chilli dip.

CRUMB-FRIED or BATTER-FRIED COTTAGE CHEESE

8 oz. cottage cheese cut in cubes

Method

Follow the same method as crumb fried/batter fried roe. Serve hot with tea or coffee or drinks with any sauce, pickle, chutney, or dip. Do not cook cheese before frying

----

BATTERED BREAD SNACKS

Bread slices as required

½ cup cottage cheese

½ tsp. coriander powder

¼ tsp. hot paprika/any chilli powder

½ tsp. *chat masala* (optional)

1 tblsp. fresh coriander leaves chopped

4-6 tblsp oil for frying

1 cup chickpea flour (*besan*)

1-2 egg whites (optional)

½ tsp. cumin powder

A pinch of *ajowan* (ptychotis)

Salt and pepper to taste

Water for the batter

Method

Combine all the above ingredients except the bread slices and oil. Make a batter with just enough water – should be of a thick dropping consistency. Remove crusts from the bread slices. Cut them in half in the shape of triangles. Dip the bread triangles in the batter to coat thickly. Now, deep, or shallow fry in a non-stick fry pan. Serve hot with a mint/coriander chutney.

Any other ingredient of choice can be added to the batter – spices, herbs, sauces, pastes, etc.

FLAVOURED COTTAGE/CREAM CHEESE ON TOAST

(Homemade or store-bought cottage/cream cheese (*paneer*) flavoured with the following suggestions, or any other substitute can be used on toasted bread/crackers or cocktail biscuits and served for supper or teatime/cocktail snacks.)

First Method:

1 cup cottage cheese	1 tblsp. fresh dill chopped
2 tsp. cream or, 1 tblsp. butter softened (both optional)	1 tblsp. thick prawn juice* or, 2-3 boiled medium prawns chopped
¼ tsp. mustard powder or paste	1-2 tsp. mustard (optional)
1 tblsp. mayonnaise	Salt and pepper to taste

First Method

Combine all the above ingredients. If served as a snack spread on cocktail biscuits or on bread slices from which the crusts have been trimmed. Cut each slice into half or quarters depending on the size and then toast on a griddle before spreading with the cheese mixture. As a supper snack apply spread generously on whole slices of toasted bread or on crackers. Serve hot. Garnish the cocktail snacks with chopped dill or a bit of chopped prawn.

Note: For prawn juice, use the water in which prawns have been boiled. Alternately boil the prawn heads in sufficient water to get a thick consistency. Strain and use for flavouring. Store excess in the freezer for future use.

Second Method:

4-6 slices of bread	1 tblsp. butter (optional)
1 tblsp. English/French mustard	Salt and pepper to taste
4-6 slices of cottage cheese	1 tsp. garlic powder
1 tsp. white cumin	1 small tomato cut in slices or chopped

Second Method

Trim the sides of the bread carefully. Spread with butter if using. Next spread a little mustard and then sprinkle salt and pepper. Place a slice of cheese. (If butter is not used then spread the cheese with the mustard if using, and salt and pepper.) Sprinkle garlic powder on top and then a few whole cumin seeds. Top with a slice or chopped tomato. Toast under the grill or place in a hot oven for 3-4 mins. A good supper snack. For cocktails cut the slices in four.

Variation:

Crumble the cottage cheese and soften with the butter or a little milk or sour cream. Mix with the mustard if using, garlic powder, whole cumin, salt, and pepper and chopped tomato. Garnish with a bit of tomato placed in the centre. Alternately a slice of tomato can be placed on top of the cheese. (In place of garlic powder, 2-3 cloves of garlic dry roasted and crushed can be substituted.) Use the garlic according to taste.

COTTAGE CHEESE PANEER SPREAD

½ cup cottage cheese (homemade or store bought)

½ tsp. (more or less to taste) garlic powder

Spring onions/tomatoes for garnish

Salt and pepper to taste

Method

Mash cheese with a fork or in the food processor till smooth and soft. Blend in the seasonings and garlic powder with the cheese. Store in a jar in the refrigerator (freezer if to be kept for more than 3-4 days) till required. Spread on cocktail biscuits or toasted/grilled bread squares. Garnish with a sprinkling of chopped spring onions or a sliver of tomato on top. A good cocktail/teatime snack.

Variation:

Combine cottage cheese with any or a combination of the following suggestions – finely chopped tomatoes, chopped cooked plain/smoked ham finely minced onions/spring onions. In place of garlic any of the following flavourings may be added – soya sauce, ketchup, Worcester sauce, chilli sauce or any other sauce of choice.

If garlic powder is not readily available, roast garlic cloves till golden brown and then pound in a mortar and pestle/ garlic crush/mini food mill without adding water.

COTTAGE CHEESE SNACKS

250 gm. cottage cheese	2-4 tblsp. mayonnaise
1 tsp. garlic powder	2-3 stems spring onion chopped fine
1 small capsicum chopped fine	1 tblsp. chives/dill chopped fine (optional)
Salt and pepper to taste	1 tsp. mustard powder/prepared (optional)

Method

Mix all the above ingredients to a smooth paste. Spread on lightly toasted bread - squares, halves or full slices with crusts removed. Before serving, place under the grill till a golden brown.

KHASTA FISH PUFFS

Fish Filling:

1 kg. fish – steamed, flaked, deboned	2 large onions – chopped
1 tblsp. oil	1 heaped tsp. each ground cumin and coriander
2 heaped tblsp. tomato purée	1 medium chopped green pepper
125 gm. Cooked green peas	125 gm. Bamboo shoots
2 eggs scrambled	Can either use all or any of the last four ingredients at your choice.
1 tblsp. Liquidized ginger	

Pastry:

500 gm. Flour	1 tsp. salt
250gm. Shortening e.g. vegetable-ghee or butter or oil or ½ lard and ½ vegetable ghee.	Cold water to mix

Method

Fry fish and onions in oil till both have a nice golden-brown colour. Stir continuously. Add the rest of the ingredients in their respective order. Cook till well mixed and no more fishy smell. Add salt to taste. Keep aside.

Sift flour and salt. Rub-in shortening. Add enough cold water, to get a soft pliable dough – not sticky. Cover with cloth and rest in refrigerator for 30 minutes. Roll pastry 1/8" thick and cut into large saucers. Put filling at one edge. Fold over saucer into a half-moon. Shape, seal edges by pressing down with fingers. Cut edges with a pastry cutter to get an even pattern. There should be altogether 12 to 16 good sized puffs.

The final cooking may be done in three ways:

1. Brush tops with milk. Bake in hot oven for 25-30 minutes till golden brown.

2. Shallow fry on a griddle or non-stick pan on low heat, till both sides brown. The griddle or non-stick pan should be only brushed with oil.
3. Deep fry in hot oil quickly to golden.

I prefer the second method for the best results. It is easier to handle, less oil, more economic and tastier.

This can also be served as a small lunch or dinner snack with "summer vegetables" or a "tomato salad" — both given in the vegetarian section of this book.

Make puffs smaller in size if serving with drinks/cocktails.

FISH KATCHURI

1 cup flour	1 heaped tsp. shortening (preferably lard or any vegetable shortening)
Water to bind	Salt

Method

Casing:

Sift flour and salt. Mix with shortening till like breadcrumbs. Add water gradually to make a pliable dough. Let rest for ½ hour covered with a bowl. Divide dough into two portions. Roll one portion at a time into a large round 1/8" thick on a smooth surface. Cut into rounds with a teacup of average size or with a cookie cutter of the same size. Put filling in each round and cover with another round. Seal by pressing down the edges — use a little water to seal if necessary. Cut edges with a pastry cutter. Deep fry.

Filling:

250 gm. Fish – steamed, deboned, and mashed	1 large onion
¼ tsp. turmeric powder	2 tsp. ketchup
½ tsp. coriander	1 tsp. oil
½ tsp. ground cumin	

Method

Cook fish in oil with all the above ingredients

Variations

1. Shallow fry till well browned on both sides. This is better done, on a griddle or a non-stick pan on low heat.
2. Brush top with milk or egg yolk. Bake in hot oven till golden. If baking, use 2 tbsp. shortening.

Note: Make smaller katchuries for drinks/cocktails.

KHASTA SINGARA

12 oz. flour

5 oz. any vegetable fat

Any filling as desired

½ tsp. salt

Water for mixing dough

4-6 tblsp. oil for frying

Method

Sift flour and salt. Add the fat and mix till almost like breadcrumbs. Add enough water to make a firm dough. Divide dough into two or three portions for easier handling. Take each portion and form into a long sausage. Take off bits from the sausage and roll in the palms of the hand into small balls the size of a "ping-pong" ball. These may be slightly larger or smaller. Place each ball one at a time on a floured board. Pat top with a rolling pin and then roll out to a round about ¼" thick. Lift gently to the palm and fold into a three-cornered cone. Put filling in the hollow of the cone and then seal the edge by crimping or with a little water. Put oil in a non-stick pan and shallow fry the *singaras* in batches, on low heat till golden brown and crispy. Serve hot with any chutney, sauce, pickle etc.

The filling can be made from any left-over food e.g. curry, minced steak, two or three combinations of curries (vegetarian, non-vegetarian.), lentil dried off etc. etc. Filling can also be made from scratch according to taste.

JAMS, PICKLES, SQUASHES, AND SAUCES

SIMPLE QUICK EASY ORANGE MARMALADE

5 lb. tight oranges

5 lb. sugar

1 cup water

20 limes juiced

Method

Peel the oranges and reserve the peel. With a pair of kitchen scissors cut the peel of oranges into thin strips. Remove threads from the orange segments. Take out the pips and tie in a cloth. Pressure cook the orange segments, bundle of pips, peel and water all together for about 15 minutes. When cool transfer the pressure cooker contents except the pips into a large saucepan with the sugar and mix well. Squeeze the liquid from the pips as much as possible into the saucepan and discard the pips. Add lime juice. Cook all on high heat for about 30 minutes till most of the liquid has evaporated. Cool and store in a sterilized 400-500 gm. jam jar.

GOOSEBERRY JAM (I)

4 lb. gooseberry   4 lb. sugar

1 pt. water

Method

Cook gooseberry and water on low heat for approximately ½ hour to 45 minutes stirring from time to time and mashing the berries with the back of the spoon. Add the sugar and mix well. Increase the heat and cook rapidly for another 20–30 minutes. Cool and store in sterilized jars.

GOOSEBERRY JAM (II)

4 lb. gooseberry

1 cup lime juice

5 oz. water

4 lb. sugar

Method

Pressure cook the gooseberry and water for 10 minutes. When cool transfer to a large saucepan. Add the lime juice and cook rapidly on high heat for about 20 minutes stirring frequently and mashing the berries with the back of a spoon. Add the sugar and mix well. Cook for another 15 minutes. Reduce heat to medium and continue cooking for approximately another 20–30 minutes till it begins to get thick. The jam will set more once it is cool. Do not dry off the liquid too much or it will not spread. Cool and store in sterilized jars.

Variation:

Gooseberry Jelly: If there is too much syrup in the gooseberry jam when making a gooseberry pie or tart drain the excess liquid and boil it down fast till it starts gelling about 20-30 minutes. Makes a good jelly for spreading on bread, muffin, scones, or cake.

PEAR JAM

4 lb. pears peeled and chopped	3 lb. sugar
1 cup water	8 limes

Method

Pressure cook the pears with the water for about 10 minutes. Let the pressure drop and then cool before opening pressure cooker. Puree pear in a blender or food processor if necessary. Add the sugar and juice from the limes. Cook over low to moderate heat till done. The extra liquid should disappear, and the mixture should reach a jam like consistency. Cool, and store in sterilized jam jars.

Variation:

If desired add 2 tblsp crystallized ginger finely minced with the sugar for a **Ginger Pear Jam**. Alternately can add 2-4 tsp ginger powder.

PINEAPPLE JAM (I)

5 lb. pineapple peeled and chopped   1 cup water

5 lb. sugar   8 limes

1-2 tsp. ginger powder (optional)

Method

Pressure cook pineapple with the water for 20–30 minutes. Let the pressure drop. Cool and then purée in a blender or food processor. Place in a heavy bottomed saucepan with the sugar, juice from the limes, ginger powder and cook on low to medium heat till reaches a jam consistency. Store in sterilized jam jars. Can use 1-2 tblsp finely chopped crystallized ginger in place of ginger powder. This quantity should make 2 jam jars.

PINEAPPLE JAM (II)

¾ kg. of sugar per kg. of pulp

5 medium ripe pineapple pulp (left over from the pineapple squash)

½ tsp. potassium-meta-bisulphate

½ tsp. sodium benzoate

25 gm. citric acid per kg. of pulp

Method

Cook the sugar and pulp together till the sugar dissolves. Add the citric acid and cook some more till jam like consistency. Take off heat and cool. Now add the potassium to prevent fermentation and sodium to prevent fungus. Stir all once properly, to mix. Store in sterilized bottles and seal till required.

GUAVA JELLY

10 lb. guava cut in small pieces

1 litre water

4 lb. or more sugar

8-10 (depending on the size) lime squeezed

Method

Pressure-cook the guavas with ¼ litre water for ½ hour. When cool add the rest of the water. Cook a little more on high heat with the lid off. Strain overnight tied in a muslin or cheesecloth or in a stainless steel or plastic colander letting the liquid drip in a container. Next day measure the liquid and add ¾ cup sugar to every cup of liquid. When the sugar dissolves add the lime juice. Alternately add 1 tblsp commercial lime juice concentrate to each cup of liquid. Cook liquid and sugar rapidly, stirring frequently till jelly forms – approximately 15 minutes. The jelly should be ready if it sets when dropped on a plate. When cool the jelly will harden more. It should be taken off the heat before it gets too thick. Guava jelly should be of a consistency which can be spread easily on toast, scones etc. When the jelly is cool store in sterilized bottles and seal till required.

GUAVA CHEESE

Method

The guavas discarded after pressure cooking for the guava jelly is used in this recipe for the guava cheese, which is thicker and more set almost like cream cheese. Put the discarded guava into a food processor and process into a fine pulp. Add ¾ cup of sugar to each cup of pulp and cook stirring continuously till the mixture is thick. During the last stage of cooking add 1 tblsp of lime juice to each pound of pulp. At this time, also add a drop of red food colouring to get a light red tint. When guava cheese is ready cool and then wrap in rounds, squares, oblongs, or any other shape in grease-proof paper. Next pack in foil and store in the refrigerator.

PEANUT BUTTER

1 kg. shelled peanut

1-2 tsp. salt or, according to taste (optional)

Method

Dry roast the pea nuts on a griddle till an even golden brown. When cool, rub between the palms to remove the skins of the pea nuts as much as possible. Some of the skins may remain. Put the peanuts with the salt if using, in a heavy-duty food processor and process till the oil from the peanuts appear and the whole reaches a creamy consistency. It may be necessary to give the processor a rest from time to time to prevent the machine from getting too over heated.

Variation:

For a honey peanut butter add 2-4 tblsp (or according to taste) plain or flavoured honey to the butter while processing. Alternately, fill 2 or 3 jars three quarter full (or as required) with the butter. Insert 2 or 3 straws inside the butter in the jars. Now pour honey or, any other syrup gently ¾ way up into the straws. Remove the straws carefully and seal jars.

Home-made peanut butter is more fun to eat. With a little bit of imagination various flavours can be incorporated into it.

LEMON GINGER JUICE

2 litre water

9 lb. sugar

1 lb. ginger minced

2 litre lemon juice

1 tsp. any preservative (available at any chemist's shop)

Method

Boil water and sugar till like syrup. Add the ginger and lemon juice and keep boiling. Lastly add the preservative and continue to boil a little longer till thick and liquid quantity reduced. Take off heat, cool and strain through a cheesecloth or muslin. Pour into sterilized bottle/s and seal till required. It is best to refrigerate once the bottle is opened. If no preservative is used, then store in the refrigerator. This is a concentrate. It can be mixed with plain water or barley water before serving.

WOOD APPLE (*BAËL*) SQUASH

2 wood apples

4 tsp. citric acid

2 cups (more or less) sugar

4 lemons

2 litres water

Method

Take out the pulp from the wood apples and process in a food processor until smooth. Add juice from the 4 lemons, citric acid, water, and sugar. Mix all and then bring to the boil. Continue boiling on high heat stirring all the time for 15-20 minutes. Remove from heat and cool. Strain and store in a bottle. Keep in the refrigerator till required. If too strong dilute with water before serving like any other squash. Add a few cubes of ice to the jug or glass if desired. A good drink for the summer.

PINEAPPLE SQUASH

5 medium ripe pineapple chopped roughly

6½ kg. (approximately) sugar

10 gm. potassium-meta-bi-sulphate

Water as required

150 gm (approximately) citric acid

Method

Process the chopped pineapple to a pulp. Strain tied in a muslin cloth to extract the juice without squeezing too much. Hang the muslin loosely tied to the faucet over the sink and let the residue juice drip into a bowl. Alternately put the pineapple in a juice extractor. Measure the liquid and keep aside. Boil separately an equal amount of water and double the amount of sugar. Add the citric acid (approx. 25 gm. to 1 litre of juice). Let the liquid boil a couple more times stirring frequently. Take off heat, cool and then strain through a muslin cloth. Add the pineapple juice and boil the whole amount together once more. Cool and add the potassium meta bi sulphate (approx. 3 gm. per litre of juice). Store in clean sterilized bottles and seal till required. Before serving add water and ice like any other squash.

Variation:

For extra flavour ginger powder may be added if desired. For every litre of squash add 1 tblsp (or according to taste) ginger powder with the pineapple juice.

Note. ¼ tsp. potassium meta-bisulphate = 5 gm. (available in any chemists or grocers)

QUICK WHITE SAUCE

1 tblsp. flour

1 tblsp. butter/margarine

¼ tsp. paprika (optional)

1½-2 cups milk

¼ tsp. nutmeg

Salt and pepper to taste

Method

Mix all the above ingredients in a saucepan using enough milk depending on the required consistency of sauce. Cook mixture on high heat whisking continuously till well blended. Lower heat and simmer stirring continuously with a wooden spoon for 5-10 minutes or till desired consistency is reached. There should be no lumps in the sauce.

Note: For a **Cheese Sauce** add 1-2 tblsp of grated cheddar/parmesan/any other mild or strong cooking cheese to the hot white sauce immediately after taking saucepan off the heat. Stir to blend.

For a richer sauce, stir in 1 or 2 egg yolks with the milk making sure the sauce does not curdle.

EASY BROWN SAUCE

1 tblsp. flour

1 bouillon cube

1 tsp. Worcestershire or any dark flavouring sauce

2 tsp. margarine or oil

1 cup or more hot water

Salt to taste

Method

Brown flour in margarine/oil without burning. Dilute bouillon cube in hot water and add to flour, stirring continuously till thick and desired consistency is reached. Add sauce and salt. Stir to mix.

Note:

Any stock may be used instead of bouillon cube and water.

TAHINA SAUCE (MIDDLE EASTERN)

8 oz. white sesame seed paste (tahina)   8 oz. water

3 fat cloves of garlic (more or less) chopped fine   1 tsp. salt

2 lemons juiced

Method

Mix all the above ingredients together in a blender or food processor till smooth. Store in a sterilized jar and refrigerate. This makes an excellent salad dressing or dip. The water content may be reduced according to taste.

BEER SYRUP

(This is great for serving with pancakes or any other desserts or cakes according to taste. Left over beer is ideal for this – cooked with sugar to get a syrupy consistency.)

  1 cup beer   2-3 tblsp. sugar

Method

Boil the above together briskly till resembles a syrup. Serve over pancakes or a favourite dessert/cake either hot or cold. Adds a deliciously novel flavour.

MOCK CREAM

½ cup soya beans

2 cups iced water

2 tsp. fresh lemon juice strained

A pinch of salt

2 cups milk powder – low fat or full cream

½-1 cup castor sugar (optional)

½ tsp. cream of tartar

1-2 tsp. vanilla essence

Method

Soak soya beans in cold water for about ½ hour. Next rub with both palms to take off the outer transparent skin. Dry beans completely with paper towel or tea towel. Next steam in a steamer or pressure cooker till soft. Take out any remaining skin. Next grind in a kitchen machine or put in a food processor till smooth. Blend or process with the rest of the ingredients and beat well till thick and creamy. Store in the refrigerator till required. The sugar quantity can be varied according to taste. This is a good accompaniment for any dessert that requires cream.

MOCK SOUR CREAM

1 small (approx. 4 oz.) can cream   1 tblsp. plain unsweetened yogurt

Method

Mix the above together and keep aside for a couple of hours or till like sour cream. Store in the refrigerator or in the freezer if not to be used for some time.

Fresh cream may also be used in place of canned cream.

DESSERT SAUCES

(Here are recipes of a few dessert sauces and fillings which make good accompaniments for desserts or ice-creams. The sauces may be thickened according to the requirement and can be used as fillings for cakes, pies, tarts, pancakes etc.)

(a) Strawberry Sauce

12 cup sugar	1 tblsp. corn flour (can be decreased or increased according to the desired constituency).
A pinch of salt	½ cup boiling water
½ cup fresh cream	1 cup strawberry juice (fresh or concentrate)

Method

Mix all the dry ingredients. Add to the boiling water and keep boiling for 5 mins. Cool. Add the strawberry juice and stir. Last of all add the cream and stir gently. Cool in the refrigerator till required.

(b) Vanilla Sauce

½ cup sugar	1 tblsp. corn flour or, according to required consistency
1 cup boiling water	½ cup fresh cream
2 tblsp. butter	A few grains nutmeg
1 tsp. vanilla essence or, pods powdered	A pinch of salt

Method

Proceed the first two steps as the strawberry sauce. Remove from heat. Stir in butter, nutmeg, and vanilla. Let cool. Gently fold in the cream and refrigerate till required.

(c) Chocolate Sauce (I)

2 tblsp. cocoa powder	4 tblsp. hot water
¼ tsp. salt	1½ cup condensed milk
1 tsp. vanilla essence	

Method

Mix the cocoa and hot water till well blended. Add the salt, stir. Add the condensed milk and stir over a pan of hot water or use a double boiler till well blended and thick. Now add the vanilla essence and more boiling water if desired and continue stirring over a pan of hot water till it reaches the right consistency. If too thin, can be thickened with a little corn flour.

(d) Chocolate Sauce (II)

200 gm. plain milk chocolate	½ cup hot water
2 tblsp. powdered milk	A pinch of salt
2 tblsp. or less sugar	1 tsp. vanilla essence
½ cup fresh cream	1 tblsp corn flour (optional)

Method

Melt the chocolate in a double boiler or over a pan of hot water. Do not let it burn. Add the hot water, milk powder, salt and sugar if using. Keep stirring till thick and well blended, and the right consistency is reached. If necessary, thicken with the corn flour at this stage. Add the vanilla. Take off heat and let it cool. Fold in the fresh cream gently. Refrigerate till required.

Note Sauces such as orange, lemon or any other fruit sauces can be made following the above recipe for strawberry sauce. Follow the recipe for chocolate sauce-1 for a coffee sauce. Use 1 tblsp or less/more instant coffee powder. A little bit of imagination and there is no end to sauces – all that has to be done is to adjust the ingredients and the quantity.

CATSUP

14 oz. tomato paste/purée	½ tsp. nutmeg powder
½ tsp. clove powder	½ tsp. ginger powder
½ cup fine sugar	½ cup red vinegar
¼ tsp. cayenne powder	½ cup (approx.) water if necessary
Lemon juice to taste	Tabasco or substitute according to Taste (optional)

Method

Mix all the above and pour into a sterilised bottle. Refrigerate and use as and when necessary. Do not keep catsup for too long if water s used.

TOMATO PURÉE

(There are a variety of tomato purées in the market. However, there is nothing like home made fresh tomato purée. So, try making your own with the following recipe and note the difference.)

1 kg. red ripe tomatoes chopped roughly	Salt according to taste
1 very large onion chopped	1 tblsp. red vinegar
1 tblsp. sugar	Bouquet garni*

* Bouquet garni is made with seasonal fresh herbs tied together with a string or, a piece of muslin. Dried herbs may be used in extreme cases. Seasonal herbs could be 1 bay leaf, 1 sprig thyme, 1 sprig parsley, 1 small piece celery. Other similar herbs may be substituted depending on the flavour required. It is best to tie the lot in a piece of fine muslin and hang it over the side of the pan. This way it is easier to remove after the cooking is over and the purée is infused with the flavour required.

Method

Put tomatoes and onion in a saucepan and bring to the boil. Add the rest of the ingredients including the bouquet garni. Lower heat and simmer for 20-30mins. When it becomes nice and thick or puree consistency, take off heat, cool and put through a blender or food processor till smooth. If necessary, return to heat to thicken a little more. Cool and store in jars with tight lids. Use as and when necessary.

TOMATO CHUTNEY

(This type of chutney is normally served after a Bengali meal before the dessert)

1 tsp. oil	½ tsp. *panchphoron* or, whole mustard seeds
500 gm. tomato peeled and chopped small	1 cup sugar
A pinch of salt	Juice of 2 large lemons
1 tsp. thin slivers of ginger or, 1 tsp. powdered dry ginger	1 cup water or less

Method

Heat oil. Add '*panchphoron*' or, mustard seeds. Add tomatoes and fry well. Now add the sugar and salt. When the sugar is dissolved add the water and cook. When the chutney begins to thicken add the ginger slivers and lemon juice. Cook for a further 1-2 minutes. Take off heat, cool and refrigerate.

Variation:

150 gm. each of apricots or prunes or both together can be added with the tomatoes. When chutney is finished sprinkle ½ tsp freshly roasted cumin powder on top of chutney and serve.

KHARISA (ASSAMESE BAMBOO SHOOT PICKLE)

(This is a great favourite in Assam. Fish cooked with *kharisa* is absolutely delicious. It can also be used as a pickle.)

250 gm. bamboo shoots pounded   1 tsp. salt

¼ cup or less water   3-4 dry red chillis

1-2 tsp. mustard powder   ½ cup (more or less) mustard oil

Method

Coat bamboo shoots with salt. Put in a jar with just enough water to cover. Do not put too much water. Cover jar and leave bamboo shoot to ferment in the open air (sun if possible) for a few days. If the weather is good and sunny it will ferment quicker. When ready add the chillis and mustard seeds. Pack the jar with mustard oil to cover and soak the bamboo shoots. Leave in the sun for a couple of days or more. The pickle is now ready. The longer the pickle is kept in the sun the better the taste

Note: Cook a fish curry the usual way by using ginger, onion paste, and *kharisa* sautéed in oil (preferably mustard) before adding the fish

----

PORK PICKLE

1 kg. pork	2 cups or more good red vinegar
1 tblsp. coriander	2 tblsp. cumin
2 tsp. fresh black mustard	½ tsp. fresh fenugreek
1 tblsp. or less fresh chilli powder	1 tblsp. garlic paste
1 tblsp. ginger paste	½ cup mustard or good white oil
1-2 tblsp. salt	

Method

Wash the pork with a little vinegar and pat dry with kitchen towel. Set aside. Roast all the dry ingredients without oil and then grind to a smooth paste with 1 cup vinegar. Similarly dry roast the garlic and ginger and grind with ¼ cup vinegar. Warm oil and fry the garlic ginger paste till red. Add all the other pastes and fry well stirring continuously. Add the pork and continue frying. Do not let the meat and paste get burnt. If paste sticks to the bottom of the pan add a little vinegar from time to time and keep scraping, turning the meat and stirring. Do not use water at any time. When there is no more lingering raw smell, and a nice aroma emanates add ½ cup vinegar and the salt. Cook till meat is done. Should take 20-30 minutes. Cool and store in clean, sterilized, dry jars. Properly made this pickle should keep for a long time without refrigeration.

MUMMY'S VINDALOO or MEAT PICKLE

1 kg. pork, venison, chicken, mutton, or beef

1½ cup good red vinegar

4 tblsp. ginger paste

1 tblsp. garlic paste

1½-2 cups mustard or good white oil

1 tblsp. fresh red chilli powder

1-2 tblsp. salt or, to taste

1 tblsp. sugar

Method

Cut the meat into cubes as in stews or curries. The meat should be boneless except in the case of chicken where the major bones could be left. However, if possible, it is always better to take the bones out. Use only the breast and legs of the chicken which should be cubed small and not left in large pieces. Wash well in vinegar, pat dry with kitchen towel and then spread on a flat tray or dish. The ginger and garlic pastes should be made fresh with vinegar. As in the previous pork pickle recipe no water should be used in the pickle at any time. Heat oil to smoking, especially if using mustard oil. Take off heat for a few seconds (to prevent spluttering) and add all the ground spices and chilli powder. Return to heat and keep frying, stirring continuously till there is a nice aroma and the spices separate from the oil. Add the salt and next the meat. Stir to coat the meat with the spices and cook for a while with continuous stirring. Mutton and beef will take a little longer to cook than pork, venison, or chicken. When almost half cooked add the vinegar and sugar, stir, and let cook till done stirring from time to time. It should become semi dry – pickle consistency. When done take off heat and cool. Store in clean dry bottles. If properly done this pickle keeps for a long time. No refrigeration required.

Note: This is best made with venison which alas is not available being a prohibited item. In the absence of venison either pork, beef, or chicken, in that order, would be the next best option

----

MISCELLANEOUS RECIPES

SANGRIA (I)

1 cup sugar	½ cup water
¼ tsp. powdered cinnamon	1 lemon
1 orange	1 large banana
2 pt. any red wine	Ice

Method

Boil sugar, water, and cinnamon together for 5 minutes and then let the syrup cool. Peel and cut the fruits into thick slices and cover with the cooled syrup. Chill for several hours. Put some ice in a glass pitcher. Add the fruit, ½ cup of the syrup and the wine. Stir and mix well slightly mashing the fruit. Serve in cold glasses. Can garnish with a few mint leaves and a cherry on a cocktail stick. An excellent drink to serve at a lunch party on a hot day.

BATIDA de LIMAO (BRAZILIAN DRINK)

6 cups fresh lemon juice

3-4 tbsp. sugar or, to taste

3 tblsp. crushed ice

6 cups water

6 cups vodka

Extra ice cubes

Method

Mix all the above ingredients except ice cubes in a tall jug or shaker. Pour in individual tumblers or cocktail glasses and serve. Add ice cubes to each glass according to taste when serving. A cool drink for the summer or a winter pre-lunch drink. May also be served during the day while relaxing or as a hot summer sundowner!! Anyway - it is a wonderful drink to make you feel just right and merry!

GLÖGG (SWEDISH HOT CHRISTMAS DRINK)

1¼ cup any alcoholic spirit (optional)

3 tblsp. Madeira

½ cup almond blanched, shredded and sliced

5-7 cardamoms skinned and crushed

4-6 whole cloves

2-3 cinnamon sticks

½ cup raisins

¼ tsp. ginger powder

A pinch of ground nutmeg

2-3 fresh/dried figs cut in squares

¼ of dried orange peel grated

1 cup water

1 bottle any ordinary red wine

Method

Mix together all the ingredients except wine and boil for 5-10 mins. Filter through a strainer. Take out the almonds and raisins and place in a clean pan. Pour the filtered liquid over it. Last of all pour the wine overall. Heat over low heat. Serve hot.

Note. If using pure alcohol, then use half water and half pure alcohol.

SOUTH INDIAN LASSI

2 cups unsweetened yogurt

A pinch of asofœtida powder

Salt to taste

1-2 fresh green chillis

1-1½ cups water

2 tsp. sugar

3-4 fresh curry leaves

Shaved ice cubes

Method

Blend yogurt, water, asofœtida, sugar and salt in a blender. Add curry leaves and chillis. Store in refrigerator till required. Before serving take out the curry leaves and chillis. Add shaved ice and serve immediately.

FEIJOADA PAULISTA (BRAZILIAN DISH)

1 kg. black beans (white beans may also be used)	½ kg. dried beef (biltong or jerky) or fillet of beef
250 gm. fresh boneless beef	2 smoked pork ribs
250 gm. fresh boneless pork	1 large or 2 medium pork sausages
250 gm. spiced or any other sausages	250 gm. bacon
½ kg. smoked pork fat	1 bulb (can use more or less) garlic crushed
(3-4 tblsp. oil may be used in preference to pork fat)	2 tblsp. chopped parsley
1 medium onion chopped	Salt and pepper to taste
2 tbsp. green onion (leek, spring onion or chives	

Method

Soak beans overnight. Next day change the water and cook the beans till tender but not too soft. If using dried meat, then boil it for a few minutes to get rid of the salt. If using fillet, then fresh beef should be omitted. Cut up all the meat, sausages and bacon into chunks or serving pieces. Cut up pork fat and heat in a pan. Alternately heat oil. Fry garlic and onions till colour changes. Add the parsley, green onions or substitute, salt, and pepper. Fry all stirring continuously for a few minutes. Add 4 ladles of the cooked beans with some of the water and mash. Add rest of the beans and all the meat, stir, and cook till all done. This serves 8 persons. Serve with thick chunks of bread.

In Rio de Janeiro this is served as above. But in Sao Palo it is served with an extra sauce as under.

Sao Paulo Sauce:

6 oz. lemon juice

6 oz. white or. red vinegar

8 oz. of the above gravy mixed with 2-3 tblsp. of the bean water

2-3 tblsp. parsley chopped

3-4 spring onion finely chopped

1 small green pepper finely chopped

Mix all the above and serve cold with the Feijoada Paulista.

PANCAKE PARTY

There is nothing like throwing a Pancake Party as a change. A stack of basic pancakes should be kept ready. The menu starts with savoury accompaniments and ends with sweet accompaniments. All that is required is a bit of imagination with a variety of fillings. Believe me, your guests will leave feeling very satisfied. Your party will be a source of conversation for them for a very long time.

Menu Suggestions for a Pancake Party:

1. A heavy soup – e.g. Goulash
2. One dish of meat (lamb, beef, chicken, or pork) filled and rolled pancakes.
3. One small dish of rolled pancakes of fish filling with an extra dish of the fish filling.
4. One dish of rolled pancakes with the shrimp filling with an extra dish of the filling.
5. One dish of cream cheese filling mixed with a little grated processed or any other cheese. Can also add chopped spring onions and/or chopped ham/bacon, chives etc.
6. One large dish of extra plain pancakes for the guests to fill and make their own rolls according to taste.
7. One bowl of green and tomato salad.
8. Dessert options
9. Round off the dinner with a bowl of fruit salad.
10. Coffee or tea.

Herewith a few recipe suggestions for your party.

Pancake Batter:

1 kg. flour	5 eggs
Salt to taste	2 tblsp. oil
1 litre (approx.) ½ milk and ½ water or,	Extra oil for frying pancakes
½ water and ½ soda water or beer	

(For sweet pancakes omit the salt and add 3 tsps. sugar. If batter is used both for savoury and sweet pancakes, just add only a little of salt – approx. ¼ tsp.)

Method

Blend all the above ingredients except the extra oil in a mixer or food processor for about 5 minutes. Brush a small non-stick frying pan or griddle (the latter will require a little more oil). Put 2 tblsp of batter in the fry pan and spread fairly thin in a circular motion or to cover the surface of the pan by tilting it around, if it is small. When bubbles start to rise, and pancake has no more sticky batter left turn it over for a few seconds till done. Make the rest of the pancakes in this manner. Line a casserole flask with a tea towel or napkin. Stack the pancakes in this and cover with the sides of the napkin or tea towel to keep them warm. Close the lid.

Fish Filling:

2 tblsp. butter	2 tblsp. heaped flour sifted
8 liquid oz. hot milk	2 egg yolks
Salt and pepper to taste	¼ tsp. nutmeg powder
1 kg. any fish boiled with salt	

Melt butter. Add flour and stir quickly till golden. (Do not let it burn). Add milk gradually and keep stirring for 2-3 minutes without letting any lumps form. Take off heat. Add egg yolks one at a time and beat. Add salt, pepper and nutmeg and stir. Last of all add the fish. Return to heat and cook for 2-3 minutes. This filling could be used for *'pantras'* or any other pie or pastry filling.

Note: 1 tsp. anchovy or fish sauce can be added with or without ketchup to the fish for a different flavour.

Shrimp Filling:

500 gm. shrimps cleaned	¼ tsp. caraway seeds
10 tblsp. level butter	2-3 tsp. paprika
Salt and pepper to taste	2 tblsp. heaped fresh cream or milk
1 bunch fresh parsley finely chopped	

Boil shrimps with caraway seeds. Throw the water away and cut the shrimps small. On low heat melt butter in a saucepan. Sprinkle paprika over it. Now add the salt and pepper. Next add the fresh cream and stir. Add shrimps and let all cook for about 1 min. Take off heat and add parsley. This can be also eaten with plain boiled rice or served as a snack on toast.

Note: A little ketchup can be added to the shrimps for extra flavour and colour.

Lamb/Beef/Pork/Chicken Filling:

Cook any of these meats according to your favourite recipe. Usually best to mince the meat. Add chopped capsicum, spring onions, chopped ginger or ginger juice, curry powder, garlic juice(optional) minced onions etc. Cook all in a little oil with a little tomato paste. Cook diced chicken with chopped mushrooms in a white sauce. Pork mince or diced could be cooked up in a Chinese manner – sweet and sour or with chopped bamboo shoots etc.

Dessert Options:

Remove all savouries from the table. Leave the stacked pancakes.

Now bring out the options -- 1 bowl of any jam, 1 bowl of fresh cream, 1 bowl of vanilla custard, 1 bowl of powdered cashew nuts mixed with castor sugar, 1 bowl of black sesame seeds mixed with icing sugar, 1 Bowl of cream cheese mixed with a little fresh cream, sugar, raisins and vanilla. If you have any other options like ice cream etc just go ahead and serve them. No need to serve all the above items – take your pick and **enjoy**!!

HUNGARIAN SAVOURY DISH

This makes an excellent all in one meal dish. However, it can be served as a first course or as the main dish. The chicken stew could be made with scraps of chicken. If made properly this dish can be most delicious!

Pancakes:

Use the recipe for pancakes from the "Pancake Party". Lessen or increase the ingredients proportionally according to the number of guests. Use two pancakes per head. Cut the pancakes into long narrow strips like pasta – tagliatelle or fettucine.

Chicken Stew:

1 kg. chicken cut in small pieces	1-2 medium onions quartered
½ tsp. black pepper	Salt to taste
2 tsp. heaped (or more) paprika	1-2 cups water
½ cup (or more) fresh cream or, yogurt	

Method

Put all the above ingredients in a heavy bottomed saucepan or pressure cooker and cook till chicken is cooked. There should be just enough water to cover the chicken. If using a pressure cooker reduce the water according to instructions. When ready take chicken pieces out of the liquid and de-bone. Add the fresh cream to the cooled liquid and stir.

Assembly:

Arrange one layer of pancake strips in a greased oven-proof dish. lay a layer chicken pieces on top and cover with the sauce. Repeat the layers once again. Cover the top with a layer of pancake strips Pour some more sauce over the pancakes. Cook in a moderate oven for approx. 20-30 minutes.

IDLI or SOUTH INDIAN STEAM-BUNS

1 cup rice   1 cup *urad dal* (black gram)

Method

Soak rice and dal separately for several hours or overnight. Drain and wash several times. Grind to a paste or put in a food processor, again separately. Now mix the two pastes together till well blended. Pour into idli moulds or in heat-proof shallow round cups. Steam or pressure- cook for about 5-10 minutes or till set. Serve the idlis with *rasam*, *sambhar* (South Indian delicacies) or any other thin curry of choice.

DOSA (SOUTH INDIAN STUFFED PANCAKES)

3 cups rice

Water for soaking batter

1 cup *urad dal* (See Oopuma)

Oil for frying dosas

Method

Soak rice and lentil in enough water to cover for 3-4 hrs. Next liquidise or put through the food processor till like a paste. Leave overnight in a warm place like a cold oven to ferment. next day put in the refrigerator till required. Take out the amount required and add a little more water to make a not too thick and not too thin batter. Warm a griddle and brush with oil (only for the first dosa). Make a very small dosa like a pancake. Rub the griddle with this dosa to take off any grime from the griddle. Next take a round spoon or ladle, fill with batter and place in the centre of the griddle. Press down with the spoon and spread the batter quite thin with a circular movement from the centre to outwards. Take 1 tsp. of oil and sprinkle around the edges. When bubbles appear and dosa is a light brown, put in the filling, fold over once like a half-moon or, thrice like a pancake. Take off heat and serve. Normally it is not necessary to turn the dosa over. If not eating immediately, keep in a warm flask. Should be served hot.

Leave the uncooked batter in the refrigerator till next required. Proceed as above.

Potato Stuffing:

1 tblsp. oil

4-5 curry leaves

250 gm. potatoes boiled, peeled, and cut up small

2-3 tblsp. water, if required

Salt to taste

$\frac{1}{2}$ tsp. whole mustard seeds

1 medium onion sliced finely

$\frac{1}{2}$ tsp. turmeric powder

1 green chilli de-seeded and sliced fine (optional)

Method:

Heat oil in a pan and put in the mustard seeds and curry leaves. When the seeds begin to splutter add the onion, fry till the colour changes. Add the potatoes, turmeric, and salt to taste. Fry all well till mushy. Add a little water only if required. Add chillis if using during the last minute of cooking.

Variation:

If the dosa batter is left too long in the refrigerator it may become too fermented. In this case, chop some onions, ginger, green chillis and/or coriander leaves. Sprinkle this mixture over the dosa on the griddle, cover and let steam. When ready uncover, fold over and serve hot.

SEMOLINA DOSA (SOUTH INDIAN PANCAKES)

2 cups fine semolina

1 tblsp. each (approx.) grated carrots, radish, green beans, cabbage, beetroot etc., etc.

½ cup approx. oil

1-2 eggs (optional)

1 tblsp. green peas

Method

Soak semolina in just enough water to cover over night. Next day put in the liquidiser or food processor and process till smooth. Add the eggs, mix, and then add the vegetables and mix all gently. Heat a griddle and brush with oil. Place batter with a round spoon at the centre of the griddle and tilt it to cover the whole surface. Turn over gently when one side is done dribbling a little oil along the sides if necessary. Continue this way till all the batter is used up. The dosas should be fairly thin. Serve with coconut, coriander or any other chutney or pickle.

(No need to use all the vegetables mentioned above. 3-4 types of vegetables of any kind that can be grated may be used.)

ARROWROOT DOSAS or SOUTH INDIAN PANCAKES

1 cup arrowroot	6 cups water
½ cup *urad dal* (black gram)	Salt to taste
1-2 tsp. (or to taste) green chilli extract (optional)	Oil as required

Method

Soak arrowroot in 4 cups water over night making sure there are no lumps. Soak the dal in 2 cups water for 2-3 hours. Drain water and use it for grinding the dal to a paste in a grinder, blender, or food processor. Keep overnight. The next day, throw away the clear water from top of the arrowroot. Add the dal paste, salt and chilli extract if using. Beat mixture well till light and fluffy. Now proceed making the dosas the same way as the semolina dosas without adding the eggs and vegetables. Serve as the semolina dosas.

Note. Green chilli extract is available in the market. However, one can easily make it at home by soaking the desired amount of green chillis for a few minutes and then squeezing out the juice or putting them in a liquidiser or food processor and then straining.

ALL IN ONE DISH

(This is basically a one dish meal with rice, meat, and vegetables. It is easy, delicious and quick to make especially for the busy housewife or the single man/woman. This is also a suitable dish to serve guests.)

500 gm. beef/mutton cut in cubes	2 tblsp. (more or less) oil
3-4 medium potatoes halved	2-3 large carrots thickly sliced
3-4 medium onions peeled and kept whole	1-2 bay leaves
6-8 cloves	3-4 green cardamoms
2" piece cinnamon	6-8 black pepper corns
1-2 onions sliced	A handful of peas (optional)
1" fresh ginger sliced (optional)	1 kg. rice preferably *'Basmati'*
2-3 bouillon cubes (optional)	4-6 cups stock
2-3 green chillis whole (optional)	Salt to taste
A handful of fresh coriander leaves	3-4 strands saffron dissolved in warm water (optional)

Method

Half cook the meat. In a deep pan heat the oil. Lightly fry the potatoes, carrots, and onions – all separately and keep aside. In the same pan heat a little more oil if necessary. Add the bay leaves, cloves, cardamoms, cinnamon, cloves, and pepper corns. When they begin to splutter add the sliced onions and brown. Add the meat cubes and brown slightly. Add all the vegetables, mix well. Now add the rice, mix all, cook for 3-4 minutes stirring continuously. Add the meat stock and more water if required. At this stage add the bouillon cubes (if using) dissolved in a little warm water. Add salt to taste and chillis, if using. Cover till rice, vegetables and meat are done and all water disappears. Sprinkle dissolved saffron and stir before taking off the heat. Garnish with fresh coriander leaves. Serve with a tomato or cucumber *raita* or salad and any hot or sweet pickle or chutney.

RECYCLING LEFT-OVER TANDOORI ROTI or CHAPATTIS

Method

Dip *roti* in a bowl of hot water to soften – not to be left too long. Place on a hot griddle sliding ½-1 tsp oil or ghee around it following the same method as in making *parathas*. Turn when one side done using a little more oil if necessary. Serve hot with any curry.

Variation:

Alternately, *chapattis* may be smeared with good, melted ghee or butter after quickly dipping in warm water. No need to place on the griddle. Stack one on top of each other in a warm dish till required. Good eating as a brunch with any dry curry or "stir fry" curry with mild spices e.g. egg, vegetables, ground meat or fish.

Note: "Left-over Roti Hulwa" see under "Sweets"

FINNISH CABBAGE PIE

Dough:

6 cups flour	½ tsp. salt
1 cup milk	1 cup oil
2 large sheets of wax paper	1 egg lightly beaten

Sift the flour and salt and mix with the milk and oil. Keep aside.

Filling:

1 (500 gm.) cabbage	1 onion chopped
300 gm. minced beef or pork	1-2 tblsp. butter or margarine
Salt and black pepper to taste	

Boil cabbage in salted water. Chop it up coarsely. Cook the onion and mince in the butter till done. Stir in the cabbage and add the seasoning. Set aside.

Divide the dough in two. On a board lay a large sheet of wax paper. Put half the dough in the centre and pat with the rolling pin to flatten. Cover with the second sheet of wax paper. Now roll the dough as large and as thin as possible. Remove the top wax paper and gently invert the dough on a flat baking tray. Remove the second wax paper. Spread filling over the dough evenly. Now proceed with the second dough in the same way. Lay it gently on the filling. Trim and seal the edges neatly. Brush top of pie with the egg. Prick surface with a fork. Bake in a hot oven till done. Cut and serve while still warm. This is good served with drinks, coffee, or tea or as hors d'oeuvres

----

KARELIAN STEAK

250 gm. pork

500 gm. lamb

5 black pepper corns

Water as required

500 gm. beef

Salt to taste

1 large onion peeled

Method

Cut all the meat into big fork size pieces. No need to discard the bones if any. Put them all together with the pork on top in a heavy bottomed oven proof pot or deep dish with the salt, pepper, and onion. Leave it like this for a few hrs. Roast in a medium low oven until the meat browns. Add water to cover the meat. Keep in the oven for about 3 hours. Serve with potatoes cooked according to taste, cucumbers, beet root or any other vegetable. The lower the oven temperature and the longer this dish remains in the oven the better the flavour.

KOUBBEH (LEBANESE NATIONAL DISH)

1 kg. very fine *borghol* or *dalia*	1 kg. lamb or beef (from the leg)
1 large onion finely minced	ground fine
Salt and pepper to taste	Water as required
2 tblsp. of butter or margarine	2 tblsp. oil

Method

The Filling:

Fry equal amount of ground meat and onion (about 250 gm. to 300 gm. in a little oil (1-2 tblsp). When done add a handful of finely chopped pine nuts. The filling should not be too oily. Keep aside till required.

Wash the *borghol* well and leave spread out on a plate or tray for about 5 minutes. Mix with the ground meat, onion, salt and pepper, and enough water to moisten and get the right consistency. The mixture should not be too dry or too wet and sticky. Form into balls the size of golf balls. Flatten balls between the palms to shape into flat round cutlets. Grease an oven proof dish, preferably round, generously with fat or butter. Place 2 or 3 cutlets or more in the dish and flatten out further with hand. Place filling on top and spread out with the back of a spoon. Once again place cutlets as above and continue in this way alternating with the filling to almost the top of the dish. The top cover as in the bottom should be the cutlet mixture. From time-to-time wet hands with water so that the mixture doesn't stick to the hands and the cutlets are smooth. When the dish is full make a hole in the centre all the way to the bottom, the size of a finger. Fill the hole with a large blob of butter or margarine. Put the rest of the butter/margarine around the sides of the koubbeh. Pour the oil all around the top of the koubbeh. Loosen the edge of the koubbeh with a knife. Bake in a medium hot oven for about ½ hr. Serve with yoghurt or/and a green, tomato or cucumber salad.

SPRING ROLLS (I)

Dough:

3 cups flour	1 cup water
A pinch of salt	½-1 tsp. oil

Method

Mix the above minus the oil and knead till slightly sticky. Brush a nonstick frying pan with very little oil only the first time. Wipe off with paper towel. With the palm of the hand wipe surface of pan with the dough very thinly. Heat pan. Remove the thin crepes when half dry by removing fry pan from the heat.

Filling:

1 tsp. oil	1 fresh ginger ground
10 cloves garlic chopped	1 cup (or more) lean pork chopped
4 small carrots cut in slivers	2 leeks cut in thin slivers
A pinch of salt	¼ small cabbage shredded
2 tblsp. light soy sauce	1 fresh green chilli – chopped fine
3 tblsp. water	

Heat oil in a deep fry pan. Add garlic, ginger and pork and mix well. Add carrots and keep stirring. Next add the leeks, pinch of salt, and stir. Add cabbage, chilli, soy sauce, water. Cover pan and allow to simmer on low heat for about 10 minutes.

Place a little filling on the inside edge of each pancake. Fold the two outer edges inwards and tuck them in by pressing down with the fingers to ensure the filling does not escape. Do not let the rolls crumble. Roll the pancakes all the way and seal with a little paste of flour and water. Shallow fry the spring rolls and serve warm. Serve with Ginger Sauce.

Ginger Sauce:

6 tblsp. water	1 cup warm water
2 tsp. tomato purée	2 tblsp. ketchup
1 cup red vinegar	3 slices ginger chopped
1 fresh hot chilli chopped	1½ tblsp. corn flour

Salt and pepper to taste

Brown sugar in a saucepan over medium heat stirring frequently. When sugar melts add the water and keep stirring till sugar dissolves once again. Add tomato puree, ketchup, and vinegar. Stir to mix. Now add the ginger and chilli stirring frequently till all well blended. Add the seasonings at this point. Last of all thicken sauce by adding the corn flour mixed with a little water to form a paste.

CHINESE SPRING ROLLS (II)

Filling:

3 medium onions sliced very thin   ½ cup oil

12-15 medium carrots shredded   ½ a large cabbage thinly shredded

Salt and pepper to taste   1 lb. pork shredded

Batter:

2 lbs. flour   1 qt. water

Method

Sauté onions lightly in the oil. Add carrots and stir to mix. Next add the cabbage, salt and pepper. Keep cooking till vegetables begin to wilt. Add the pork and stir all together. Take off heat, drain off excess oil and keep aside till batter ready.

Beat flour and water for 15-20 minutes till glossy but not sticky. Very lightly grease a heavy griddle or use a non-stick fry pan in which case oiling is not necessary. Swipe a handful of dough over the surface of griddle/pan very quickly. When the edges begin to curl peel off fast and fill. Roll up like a parcel making sure the ends are tucked in well to prevent filling from falling out. Pack carefully in foil and freeze till required. The rolls will keep for 4 months or more. When required take out and thaw. Deep fry in oil, drain on paper towel and serve hot with soy sauce or chilli sauce.

Variations:

Shrimps or shredded chicken can be substituted in place of pork. In both cases no need to pre-cook. They can be added after the onion and then followed by the vegetables used. Chives or/and bean sprouts can also be added to the vegetables at the last minute.

INDONESIAN SPRING ROLLS THE EASY WAY

Batter:

1 cup flower	½ cup potato flour/corn starch/corn flour
¼ tsp. salt	1 cup lukewarm water
1 egg	Oil as required

Filling:

125 gm. chicken/shrimp/pork	Any or all the following vegetables as desired, carrots, celery, bamboo shoots, cabbage, bean sprouts
2 large onions sliced thinly	2 fat cloves garlic sliced
2 tblsp. oil	Salt and pepper to taste
	1 bouillon cube/½ tsp. gourmet powder

Method

Sauce:

Make the sauce with ground pea nuts or peanut butter, ketchup, tabasco/chilli-powder/chilli sauce, sugar, and salt to taste. Mix all these ingredients with a little water.

Filling

Chop meat finely against the grain. Shred the larger vegetables. Fry onions and garlic in oil for 1-2 minutes. Add meat or shrimps and fry another 2-3 minutes. Next add the vegetables being used for another 2-3 minutes. Do not overcook. Add seasoning and crumbled bouillon cube/gourmet powder. Stir all to mix and keep aside till pancakes are ready.

Batter

Mix all the dry ingredients together. Beat egg and then add the dry ingredients to it. Add enough water to make a batter like pancakes of pouring consistency.

Pour batter from a jug onto a nonstick fry pan or a heavy skillet/griddle brushed lightly with oil. Make thin pancakes, put in filling roll like the Chinese spring rolls and deep fry. Drain on paper towel and serve hot with the sauce.

Note: If using a griddle/skillet, rub salt generously on the surface with a bit of paper and then throw the salt away to give it a rough edge.

SUSHI

3½ cups rice

5 tblsp. white vinegar

2 tblsp. sugar (Osaka style)

¼ cup carrots shredded

¼-½ cup bamboo shoots canned/cooked and sliced

¼ cup green peas frozen/dehydrated/fresh cooked

½ cup crab meat shredded (optional)

Red pickled ginger strips for garnishing

¾ tsp. *ajinomoto*

2 tsp. salt and 2 tsp. sugar (Tokyo style)

¼ cup green beans steamed and sliced

¼-½ cup mushrooms canned/cooked and sliced.

½ cup shrimps (optional)

Several thin omelette strips depending on the number of guests

Thin black seaweed in strips for garnishing

Method

Cook the rice with ¼ tsp *ajinomoto*. Put the vinegar in a bowl along with either the Tokyo style sugar and salt or Osaka style sugar, together with the remaining *ajinomoto*. Let this mixture rest for 15 minutes. Place the cooled rice in a bowl preferably wooden. Sprinkle mixture over rice and mix in a cutting motion. Next add all the vegetables and sea food (if using) one by one and keep on mixing in the same cutting motion. Put portions of rice on serving plates. Garnish with omelette strips topped with black seaweed and pickled ginger before serving.

TAMAGODOFU (JAPANESE)

(This is basically a Japanese set custard which can be served as an appetizer, a snack or as an accompaniment with any meat dish e.g. steak, barbecued or grilled meat etc. etc.)

5 eggs	1 cup stock fresh or, from bouillon cubes preferably chicken
1 tsp. salt to taste	½ tsp. sugar
1 tsp. *ajinomoto* or any gourmet powder	1 tsp. white wine preferably *sake*
1 tsp. Japanese soy sauce	

Method

Break the eggs in a bowl and then add the stock, soy sauce, salt, sugar, *ajinomoto* and last of all the wine. Mix well all together. Strain through a soup strainer so there are no lumps in the mixture. It should be smooth. Grease a heat-resistant mould with salad oil and then pour mixture into it. Heat water in a double boiler or steamer for about 3 minutes. Next put the mould on top of the double boiler Wrap the lid with a cloth and cover the boiler. Cook on high heat for about 3 minutes and then lower heat and cook till custard is set. The heat should not be too high, and the custard should not be over cooked or else holes will appear in the custard, which is not desirable. Follow the same method if using a steamer. When ready, let cool slightly and then place in the refrigerator to cool and set further. Turn out of the mould, cut in squares, and serve garnished with a small piece or slice of lemon.

CHOP SUEY

1-2 tblsp. peanut oil

6 oz. meat (lamb or beef) cut in thin strips

5 oz. bamboo shoots cut in thin strips

3 oz. mushrooms cut in wide thin strips

3 oz. water chestnuts cut in thin strips (optional)

5 oz. bean sprouts

1 tsp. Japanese light soy sauce

¾ cup water

½ lb. thin Chinese egg noodles or spaghetti

¼ tsp. gourmet powder or, ajinomoto (optional) or a pinch of sugar

2 tsp. corn flour

Method

In a deep wide pan or a wok, heat 1 tblsp. oil. Stir fry the meat strips quickly stirring continuously. Keep aside. Add the rest of the oil to the pan and stir fry all the vegetables till done. Add meat and sauce. Stir once. Mix the corn flour and water and add to the meat and vegetables and stir well to mix thoroughly. Add the gourmet powder now, if using. It should not be too squashy or lumpy.

Cook the noodles as per instructions and stir fry in a little oil before adding to the meat and vegetables. Check for salt.

Variation:

Instead of lamb and beef substitute the following – 6 oz. of chicken from the breast cut in thin strips and 4 oz. pork cut in thin strips or, 4 oz. cooked, smoked, or plain ham cut in wide thin strips. Continue as above. If using cooked ham, add at the last stage of cooking before adding the corn flour mixture.

ORIENTAL MEAT LOAF

8 oz. lamb or beef or, a combination of 4 oz. chicken and 4 oz. pork/smoked/plain ham

4 oz. mushrooms minced

2-3 eggs

Salt and pepper to taste

1 tsp. sesame oil

4 oz. water chestnuts minced

2-3 spring onions chopped fine

1 tsp. soy sauce

5 oz. corn flour

½ medium capsicum chopped fine

Method

Mince all meat and vegetables. Add the rest of the ingredients except oil and mix well. Grease a loaf pan or any other baking tray. Place meat loaf in it. Smoothen out top and drizzle with oil. Bake in moderate hot oven. When done, cool and turn out on a wire tray. Cut in slices and serve with extra soy sauce, chilli sauce and cut up chillis in vinegar. A good snack with drinks or tea/coffee.

SUKIYAKI

This dish can be made either with mutton or fillet of beef or breasts of chicken or pork OR a combination of chicken and pork or ham.

¾ cup light soy sauce	5-6 tblsp. sake, dry sherry, brandy, or beer
2 tblsp sugar	¾ cup consommé any flavour
3-4 tblsp. oil	2 lb. meat seared on a hot griddle and cut paper-thin across the grain
½ cup celery thinly sliced	2 large onions thinly sliced
5-6 oz. bamboo shoots thinly sliced	8 oz. mushrooms thinly sliced
6-8 spring onions cut thinly against the grain	8 oz. green spinach or, *bok choi* cut in pieces
½ tsp. any gourmet powder	Salt to taste
Large pinch of black pepper	

Method

Mix soy sauce, sake, black pepper, consommé, sugar, and salt, in a bowl. Marinate meat in half of this mixture. Heat oil in a skillet. Stir fry meat, drain, and keep aside. Next cook onions and celery in oil for a few minutes till they change colour. Add the rest of the marinade, meat, bamboo shoots and mushrooms and cook for another 3-4 minutes. Add the spring onions and spinach. Cook for another 3-4 minutes. Add the gourmet powder and toss all well together and serve hot.

FUYONG HAI (INDONESIAN)

2 cabbage leaves (do not use the leaves from the outer layer of the cabbage	1 tblsp. celery (tender part of the stem) or leek
4 spring onions	1 oz. pork, shrimp, chicken breast or crab minced
4 eggs	1 fat clove garlic
Salt and pepper to taste	A pinch of ajinomoto or gourmet powder
1 tblsp. soy sauce	Oil for deep frying

Method

Slice the first four ingredients fine and put in a bowl. Add any or a combination of the above meat or sea food and mix all together well. Now break the eggs one at a time and mix all thoroughly once again. Add the seasonings and soy sauce. Heat oil and deep fry the mixture by spoonfuls. Pour the following sauce over the *fuyong* and serve while still hot.

Sauce:

½ pt. ketchup	1 tblsp. soy sauce
½ cup water	2 tsp. or more corn flour
1 cup canned green peas drained	

Mix all the above ingredients and cook over low heat until thick. Stir in the peas.

OOPUMA (SAVOURY SEMOLINA DISH FROM SOUTH INDIA)

(This makes an excellent teatime snack, breakfast dish or even a light supper. For those who are strictly non-vegetarian 2-3 sausages cut small or slivers of cooked chicken or ham may be added just before cooking is complete. Stir a few times to blend well with the vegetables and semolina. This is best cooked in a wok as it will be easier to handle. If using a non-stick wok cook on high heat. Lower heat after adding the semolina.)

2 cups semolina	2 tblsp. oil
1 tsp. whole black mustard seeds	6-8 fresh or dry curry leaves (sprinkle a little water, if using the latter)
1 medium carrot cut in small cubes	2 tsp. *'urad dal'* (black gram lentil)
1 medium potato cut in small cubes	½-1 cup small cauliflower florets
1 tblsp. peas	1 medium onion sliced
1-2 whole green chillis or, de-seeded and sliced (optional)	2 cups water (¾ cups if semolina is fine)
2 tsp. ginger finely chopped	Juice of 1 small lime (optional)
A few cashew nuts roasted (optional)	Salt to taste

Method

Dry roast the semolina and keep aside. Heat oil. Add mustard seeds, curry leaves, ginger and *urad dal*. When they start to splutter add all the vegetables including the onion, add chillis, and fry till the colour changes. Add water and salt and let the whole come to boil. Add semolina and stir continuously till thick and dry. Add cashew nuts, stir a couple of times, and take off heat. Add the lime juice and serve hot.

CABBAGE SCRAMBLE EGGS

1-2 tblsp. oil for frying

1 small onion chopped

10 white cabbage leaves sliced

A pinch of ajinomoto

1 clove garlic chopped fine

Salt and pepper to taste

1 oz. pork, chicken, shrimps or, crab etc. (optional)

1 or more egg

Method

Heat oil in a frying pan. Fry garlic and onion with salt and pepper on low heat. When onion is almost done add the cabbage and keep stirring. Add the meat or sea food if using. Add the eggs at the end and keep on stirring till done. Add the ajinomoto and stir once. Serve hot.

SCRAMBLED CABBAGE WITH LEFT-OVER MEAT

1-2 tblsp. oil	1 small or ½ large cabbage shredded
2 medium carrots grated	1 or 2 onions thinly sliced
3-4 spring onions cut in thin strips	1 green or, red capsicum cut in thin strips
½" piece ginger thinly sliced	2 or 3 eggs
8 oz. (more or less) leftover meat cut into thin strips	Salt and pepper to taste
1-2 tblsp. soya sauce	A large pinch of ajinomoto

Method

Heat oil slightly in a wok and stir fry all the vegetables. When they change colour add the meat and stir. Next add the eggs one at a time and scramble with the vegetables and meat. Add the soya sauce and stir to mix. Add the seasonings and ajinomoto, stir before taking off heat.

Note. Any left-over roast grilled or barbecued meat such as lamb, beef, chicken, pork etc. can be used. Bean sprouts, bamboo shoots, mushrooms, ham bacon, sausages may also be added. Use only one type of meat. Shrimps can be substituted in place of the meat. Shrimps and the uncooked pork products will need to be cooked a few minutes longer than the cooked left-over meat. Do not overcook this dish. The vegetables should be crunchy and not limp and soggy.

LEFT-OVER FROM LEFT-OVERS!

8 oz. flour

1 tsp. baking powder

Salt to taste

2 eggs

Enough milk and water for batter

Left over scrambled cabbage

Oil for frying

Method

Sift the dry ingredients together. Add the eggs slightly beaten and then enough milk or water or half milk and half water to get a batter consistency. Let batter rest for about 10-15 minutes. If any of the scrambled egg and meat (or substitute) dish is left over, mix it in this batter and fry in a non-stick pan which requires less oil, in spoonfuls (round soup or teaspoon) or deep fry. These fritters can also be made with tempura batter. Serve with soy and chilli sauce. These fritters can be served as snacks with drinks or tea/coffee.

Note: Any other left-over meat, fish, vegetarian dish can be re-cycled in the same way.

PRESERVING VEGETABLES

Fresh Peas

Tie fresh peas in a muslin bag. Boil water with a heaped teaspoon of soda bicarbonate. Dip the bag with the peas in the boiled water for a few seconds. Take out and dry off Peas, preferably in the sun. Pack in polythene bags or wrap in aluminium foil and freeze. This retains the colour of the peas.

Bamboo Shoots

Shred bamboo shoots fine. Plunge in boiling salted water. Immediately plunge in ice cold water for a few seconds. Dry, pack in polythene bags or foil and freeze.

Other Vegetables

All other vegetables e.g. broccoli, cauliflower, carrots etc. etc can be frozen in the above method during the season and then enjoyed as and when required during the off season.

RADISH FLOWER

1 radish

1 tsp. salt

2 tsp. soy sauce

A pinch of *ajinomoto* to taste

1 cup water

3 tsp. white vinegar

½ tsp. sugar

1-2 egg yolks boiled and sieved

¼ or less red pepper chopped for garnish

Method

Peel radish very finely to give it a round shape. Balance the radish between 2 chopsticks or just plain sticks. Make thin slices without cutting right through. Turn radish round and once again slice without cutting right through from the other end. Place the radish flowers in the water with the salt for 2 hours. Take flowers out and squeeze the water out. Dip in a mixture of the vinegar, soy sauce, sugar and *ajinomoto*. Take out of the mixture and open the flowers out and press between the palms in a clockwise direction. Decorate centre of flowers with the sieved egg yolks which should resemble egg powder. Put one small piece of red pepper on top of the egg powder. Place flowers sidewise on a chrysanthemum leaf failing which on a cut lettuce or spinach leaf.

These can be placed on a tray in a buffet or as an attractive accompaniment to any Japanese or oriental *sheesh* kebab.

STUFFED BATTER FRIED PATAL/PALWAL (INDIAN VEGETABLE)

6-8 patals slightly peeled	Oil for frying
8 oz. fish steamed, de-boned and crumbled	1 large onion minced
½ tsp. cumin powder	¼ tsp. turmeric powder
¼ tsp. chilli powder (optional)	2 tsp. ketchup or, tomato paste
1 tblsp. fresh coriander leaves minced	½ tsp. coriander powder
A handful of raisins	½-1 cup gram flour (*besan*)
Salt to taste	

Method

Chop off top of *patal* and hollow out centre without damaging the vegetable. Reserve the top. Alternately slit along one side of the *patal* and take out the seeds and as much of the flesh as possible.

Prepare the filling by heating 2 tsp oil. Fry fish with the onion and spices. Add the ketchup salt, coriander leaves and seasoning. Mix well before taking off the heat. Cool and then fill the *patals* with this mixture. Place the tops of *patal* back and seal with a thick paste of flour and water. If the *patals* have been slit along the side, then tie with thread.

Make a thick batter with the gram flour and water as required. Beat batter till light and fluffy. Let it rest for 1 hour. Now dip the *patals* in this batter and deep fry. Drain on paper towel and serve hot.

Variations:

1. Any ground meat, shrimps, boiled mashed eggs or a medley of vegetables cut small and boiled before being cooked with the spices can be used in place of fish. The meat and shrimps do not require to be pre-cooked. They can be cooked with the spices straight away.

2. *Sauteed patal:* The flesh and the seeds of the *patals* can be kept aside and turned into a baked vegetable accompaniment. Brush a non-stick pan with oil and sauté 2-3 chopped onions together with the flesh and seeds

of the *patals*, 1-2 tblsp ketchup or tomato puree/paste, salt to taste, a pinch of chilli powder (optional). Cook till the onions are transparent and well mixed with the vegetable. Place mixture in an oven-proof dish, sprinkle top generously with a medium strong cheese and brown under the grill. This dish can be served with any meat, fish, vegetable as an accompaniment.

SALAD PLATTER

Method

Line a large flat dish with lettuce or tender green spinach. Next arrange any of the following ingredients in rows and pour dressing over all just before serving. Do not use too many items – 6-8 should be more than enough. Arrange them in alternate rows. Make the platter colourful and attractive by selecting and arranging the items carefully.

Suggestions for salad ingredients:

Stuffed green olives, cooked ham cubes, cheese fingers (gouda, edam etc.), hard boiled eggs cut lengthwise, tomatoes cut lengthwise, tart apple rings with skins on, cubed/sliced beetroot, pineapple cubes, sliced table radish, carrot or/and cucumber stick.

Salad Dressing:

4 tblsp. extra virgin olive oil	3 tblsp. lemon juice
1 small onion minced	1 tsp. sugar
Salt and pepper to taste	A pinch paprika (optional)

Mix all and store till required.

CHEESE SOUFFLÉ

200 gm. butter	125 gm. flour sieved
Salt and pepper to taste	½ litre milk
6 eggs separated	200 gm. parmesan cheese
300 gm. Emmenthal/Gruyere cheese	¼ tsp. baking powder

Method

Liberally grease an oven proof dish with butter. Melt butter in a saucepan. Add the flour and stir. When mixture begins to bubble add the salt. Cook till a little reddish stirring continuously. Add the pepper. The mixture should not become lumpy. Add lukewarm milk all at once, stir and take off heat. Leave pan in a bowl of cold water to cool – should not get too cold. When cold take pan out of the cold water and add the yolks all together and mix well. Add the two cheeses which have been shredded (not powdered) just before use. Again, mix all very well. Add the baking powder making sure it blends well with the mixture. Sprinkle a pinch of salt in the egg whites to make it rise well when beaten. Beat whites on low preferably with an electric hand beater. Increase speed to medium. Gradually increase speed to high and keep beating till stiff. Fold in stiffly beaten whites a little at a time to the cheese mixture.

Fill the buttered dish with the mixture. Place dish in a pan of warm (not hot) water and cook on top of the stove for about 15 minutes. After that, put in a hot oven for about 20 minutes. Alternately place in a moderately hot oven for about 15 minutes. Increase the heat to hot for about 20 minutes and then to very hot for about 10 minutes. Serve the soufflé immediately or else it will collapse. The base of any soufflé is a good béchamel sauce flavoured with Cointreau or any other liqueur, lemon extract and zest etc. etc. instead of cheese.

A well-made cheese soufflé should be light. However, it can be heavy on the stomach so either serve it as a first or main course with a green salad or as an accompaniment in small portions to any meat dish.

GROUND MEAT, CHICKEN or FISH PIE

Pastry Dough:

12 oz. flour	¼ tsp. salt
6 oz. margarine	2 yolks or, 1 (or more) whole large egg
Ice water, only if required	

Method

Mix all the dry ingredients and then cut in the margarine as in short crust pastry to resemble breadcrumbs. Add the yolks or whole eggs one at a time and mix to bind with a wooden spoon. Add just enough iced water to form into a smooth ball. Cover with a cloth and leave in the refrigerator for a while or till required.

Filling:

Any ground meat, shredded chicken or flaked fish cooked in white sauce or curried. Cooked mushrooms, peas, diced carrots can be added to the cooked fish or chicken with the white sauce and a dash of Worcestershire sauce. A little minced capsicum can also be added for extra flavour.

Alternately the above can also be curried by using any spice or a combination of spices e.g. minced onion, curry powder, coriander and cumin powders, onion and ginger paste, a little minced capsicum, shredded spring onions along with peas and cubed potatoes (optional).

Take pastry out of the refrigerator. Pat with the rolling pin. Roll out pastry on a floured board ¼ "in thickness. Cut in rounds to fit patty pans or cupcake moulds. Grease and dredge with flour the pans / moulds. Line them with rounds of pastry pulling and stretching to be even. Place filling in the pastry cases and then cover with another round of pastry sealing the edges by pressing down with the fingers. Next crimple the edges or cut with a pastry cutter to give a neat effect. Brush top of each patty with milk / yolk / egg white. Bake in a hot oven till golden or done.

Note Any leftover dish e.g. roast, grilled, baked casserole etc. meat or fish dish or curry can be used as a filling.

QUICK HAMBURGERS

Left-over curry/kebabs

Green lettuce leaves

Slice cheese

Oil as required

Hamburger buns

Sliced tomatoes

Ketchup/mustard/any other sauce of choice

Method

Make patties with leftovers. Brush a griddle with scant oil and heat patties till a golden-brown colour. Split warmed buns. Line with lettuce leaves. Place patties on top and then end with a slice of tomato and cheese. Smear with ketchup/mustard etc. Close bun and serve immediately or heat on the griddle/microwave very quickly before serving.

Variation:

Use the leftovers as a filling for *paratha* rolls. For extra flavour sprinkle the filling with chopped raw onion and green chillis (optional) or green pepper before rolling the *paratha*. Wrap rolls with grease proof paper for easy handling while eating.

QUICK and EASY PIZZA

Dough:

2 cups flour	1 tsp. salt
3 tsp. baking powder	½ cup any shortening

½ cup milk/water/combination of both

Method

Topping:

Tomatoes, cheese, mushrooms/ salami/ sausages/ ham, capsicum, oregano/ Italian seasoning/ mixed herbs etc. - any or a combination of these ingredients can be used with any of the seasonings for added flavour.

Sift all the dry ingredients for the dough in a bowl. Cut in the shortening. Add the milk and mix well and form into two balls. Turn dough one at a time onto a floured board and pat lightly with the rolling pin. Roll out resembling a pizza base Grease a nonstick griddle very lightly and place pizza round on it. When one side is cooked carefully turn over. While the underside is cooking spread the toppings selected evenly on the cooked side. Sprinkle top with a generous amount of cheese and herbs. Keep cooking till underside is done and the filling slightly set.

This can also be done in the oven or microwave in which case bake the pastry till nearly done and then arrange the topping. Assemble all as in a normal pizza sprinkling a little olive oil if desired, on top and bake in the oven a little longer till done.

MOCK LASAGNE

Pancakes:

4 oz. flour	A pinch of salt
1 egg	4 tblsp. (or more) milk
Water as required	4 tblsp. oil (more or less)

Method

Sift the flour and salt together. Add the egg and mix. Next add the milk stirring with a wooden spoon. Add sufficient water if required to get a smooth batter of pouring consistency. Brush a preferably non-stick frying pan with 1 tsp oil and then make the pancakes one at a time brushing the pan with oil only when necessary. Store the pancakes in between a sandwich cloth or cover with a tea towel till required.

Meat Sauce:

1 or 2 onions minced	8 oz. any ground meat
1 tblsp. oil	2-4 tblsp. tomato sauce or purée
1 tsp. oregano/ marjoram/ thyme/ Italian dressing	Salt and pepper to taste
2-4 tblsp. water	1 bouillon cube (optional) crumbled

Sauté the onion and meat together in the oil till both change colour. Add the purée, herb, seasoning, bouillon cube and water. Mix all together and simmer for about 5 minutes. It should be thick and a red colour.

Cheese Sauce:

1 small onion minced	2 oz. butter
2 oz. flour	1 pt. milk
Salt and pepper to taste	1-2 tblsp. mild cheese grated

In a saucepan combine the onion, butter and flour and stir over low heat till butter melts. Add the milk gradually stirring continuously till mixture well blended and there are no lumps. Take off heat, add the seasoning and cheese and mix well. Keep aside till required.

Method

Grease a round oven proof casserole. Line the base with pancake/s. Spread top evenly with some of the meat sauce and cover with some of the cheese sauce. Continue alternating with pancakes, meat sauce and cheese sauce. Finish with pancakes on top. Sprinkle top generously with grated cheese preferably parmesan. Dot with butter. Bake in a medium hot oven till done. It should be a golden brown. Serve with a green or tomato salad.

DALIA PORRIDGE

4 tblsp. *dalia (borgul)*

1 tblsp. (more or less) sugar

½ tsp. cinnamon powder (optional)

½ cup or more milk

½ tsp. vanilla essence

A pinch of salt

Method

Soak *dalia* with just enough water to cover for about 1 hr or overnight. In a saucepan cook the *dalia* with the rest of the ingredients over medium heat till thickened or the desired consistency. Serve at breakfast. The *dalia* can be cooked after soaking, with water instead of milk. Also omit the sugar. Add the desired quantity of milk and sugar at the table just before eating.

GRANOLA

(A deliciously healthy breakfast cereal)

4 tblsp. butter	1/3 cup honey
¼ cup brown sugar	1 tsp. vanilla essence
½ tsp. salt or, to taste	¼ cup water
8 cups oats	1 cup wheat germ
½ cup or less white sesame seeds	¾ cup raisins
½ cup chopped dates	¼ cup or more chopped almonds or, any other nuts

Method

Melt butter, honey, brown sugar, vanilla, salt, and water in a deep and wide oven-proof dish. Add the oats, wheat germ and sesame seeds. Mix all gently till all the dry ingredients are moist. Bake in a medium hot oven for about 20 minutes. Stir and bake once more for another 15 minutes. Continue this way 3-4 times until the mixture is ready – should be crumbly like cereal. Be careful not to let the cereal get burnt. Add the raisins, dates, and nuts before the final baking. Cool and store in an air-tight jar. Serve with hot or cold milk as a breakfast cereal or at any other time.

Any other ingredients of one's choice may be added e.g. currants, apricots, preserved cherries, figs or crystalised ginger etc. Similarly, any of the above items may be omitted e.g. sesame seeds, dates etc. The main ingredients should not be omitted.

CHOCOLATE

500 gm. sugar

13 oz. powdered milk

4 oz. margarine or, butter

8 oz. milk

3 oz. cocoa

1 tblsp. any nuts or raisins, or a combination of both (optional)

Method

Boil sugar and milk for 8-10 minutes. Mix powdered milk and cocoa together well. Add to the sugar and milk mixture. Add margarine or butter slowly and beat with an electric hand beater on 1. Add nuts, raisins etc. if using and mix slowly with a wooden spoon. Grease a rectangular or square baking tray and spread the mixture evenly onto it. Leave till set and then refrigerate. Cut into squares and store again in the refrigerator till required.

GLOSSARY

Ajinomoto	Monosodium glutamate (MSG)
Aloo	Potato
Aubergine	Brinjal or egg plant
Ahrar dal	Yellow lentil. Also known as 'tuvar'
Au gratin	A dish quoted with sauce, sprinkled with cheese and crumbs browned in oven or under grill
Barfi, burfi	Dry and sugary Indian confectionary
Bati-charchari	Another type of dry Bengali curry
Beorek	A Middle Eastern pastry dish
Bhapa	Steamed Indian food
Brinjal	Eggplant or aubergine
Bhujia	Dry fried or oven roasted mixed savoury nuts, lentils etc.
Biryani (Biriani)	A special type of 'pilau' usually cooked with meat
Borgul	Cracked wheat
Bori	Shaped and sun-dried balls or lumps of lentils
Casserole	Slow cooked food in a covered heat-proof dish in oven or the utensil itself for such
Chanchra	Bengali dry curry of assorted vegetables
Chapatti	Or roti, handmade, usually round, flat unleavened bread
Charchari	Dry Bengali vegetarian curry
Channa	Cottage cheese similar to 'paneer'

Chenchki	Another type of Bengali dry vegetarian curry
Chop suey	"Mixed spice" in Chinese – an American dish of meat (chicken, beef, pork, prawn) cooked quickly with vegetables
Cholar dal	Lentil made out of split brown peas
Crepe	Word of French origin, fine pancake
Curry powder	A mixture of various Indian spices often used for making curries (commercially available)
Daab	Green coconut
Dal	Any Indian lentil usually with the specific type mentioned before e.g., moong dal
Dalia	Broken wheat used as porridge and in various other dishes
Dalna	Bengali curry with gravy
Dárazsfeszek	Sweet pastry of Hungarian origin
Doi	Yogurt
Dolma	Stuffed vegetable
Dum	Vegetable normally cooked under pressure
Eggplant	Aubergine, brinjal
Escalopes	Flattened meat or fish
Falafel	A Middle Eastern snack
Fettucine	A type of Italian flat pasta
Flambé	A dish, sprinkled with spirit, set alight before serving
Flan	An open tart filled with fruit, cream, custard etc
Galantine	French dish with meat or poultry served cold covered with aspic

Ghonto	A 'mushy' Bengali vegetarian (sometimes non vegetarian) curried dish
Granola	Cereal mixture made of many nutritious items
Gulab jamun	A very popular fried Indian sweet in syrup, brown in colour
Hilsa	Very popular migratory ocean fish caught in the rivers of Bengal delta, akin to 'shad' of the Americas
Hulwa	Also known as Hulva. Soft Indian sweet
Jackfruit	A tropical fruit eaten raw when ripe or cooked while green as a vegetable.
Jhaal	A Bengali curry with chilli hot gravy. Also, peppery or chilli hot
Jhole	Bengali stew
Kalia	A rich and spicy Bengali curry
Kalo Jam	Indian black berry growing in a large tree, supposed to have medicinal properties
Khasta	Indian flaky pastry
Kheer	Indian milk dessert
Kitchri	A mixed rice and lentil preparation
Kochuri	Indian snack of wheat casing and vegetable, lentil (sometimes meat) stuffing usually fried in round shapes
Kofta	Ground meat, fish, or vegetable ball
Korma	A type of rich meat/fish/vegetable curry
Langosh	Or 'Langosch; Hungarian savoury cake
Lo-mien	Chinese dish with noodles, vegetables, meat, shrimps, seafood, and wontons.

Ma	My mother-in-law, Nilima Ghosh, who had a small repertoire of some very tasty dishes.
Malai	Cream of milk
Malpoa	Bengali fried sweet pancake in syrup
Methi	Fenugreek
Meringue	Small pâtisserie made from egg white and sugar
Mishti	Bengali sweets in general
Moong	A green lentil
Moussaka	A meat and egg-plant preparation of Greek origin
Mousse	A cold souffle
Mowcha	Flower of banana plant eaten all over Southeast Asia and Bengal
Mummy	My mother, Ratnavali Baruah, who was a great cook and the daughter of Pragna Sundari Devi the writer of the ground-breaking cook book in Bengali
Pakhi	My sister, Lalitha Jauhar, from whom I learned some Punjabi dishes
Paneer	Another name for 'channa' or cottage cheese
Paratha	Handmade Indian shallow fried bread
Pulao	Also known as Pilau. A rich rice dish
Rasam	South Indian sour soup and eaten as a starter
Riki	My son, Dr. Richik Ghosh; a reasonably good cook, who developed a few dishes as a student, overseas.
Roti	Chapatti or handmade, usually round, flat unleavened bread.
Rosogolla	A Bengali cottage cheese ball in syrup

Saag	Leafy green vegetable e.g. spinach
Sauerkrat	Pickled cabbage of German origin
Sambhar	A South Indian spicy lentil preparation
Sandesh	A dry Bengali confectionary sweet made mainly with cottage cheese
Singara	A pyramid shaped savoury pastry (fried or baked) usually filled with curried items. Also known as 'samosa'.
Sara	My maid, who surprised us with some of her innovations in cooking
Sembe	Swahili word meaning coarse ground maize
Sorsé	Indian mustard or 'rape' seed
Stella mashi	My mother's friend, Stella Das, and a great cook.
Sukiyaki	A dish of Japanese origin
Sushi	Any fresh raw food dish – Japanese origin
Tarkari	A dry Bengali curry
Tengri	Leg or leg bone of animals (usually goats)
Teriyaki	A Japanese cooking technique where food is broiled or grilled in a special sweet soya sauce
Thore	Soft inside of the trunk of a banana plant – a popular vegetable of Bengal (rhymes with 'more')
Tortes	Open tart or rich cake type mixture baked in a pastry case
Zucchini	A vegetable also known as courgette

ALPHABETICAL LIST OF RECIPES

Recipe	**Page**
All In One Dish	156
Anchovy Puff	66
Apple and Roquefort Cheese	65
Arrowroot Dosas or South Indian Pancakes	155
Banana Pancakes	33
Basic Scones	42
Basic Short Crust Pastry	11
Batida de Limao (Brazilian Drink)	142
Battered Bread Snacks	102
Beer Syrup	128
Beorek (I)	14
Beorek (II)	15
Beorek (III)	16
Bhakari Vadi	58
Brandy Snaps Made Easy	23
Cabbage Scramble Eggs	173
Catsup	133
Cheese Balls	49
Cheese Pakoras	48
Cheese Scones	43
Cheese Snacks	47
Cheese Soufflé	181
Cheesecake	41
Chicken Chaat	90
Chinese Fritter Batter	28
Chinese Spring Rolls (II)	163

Recipe	**Page**
Chocolate	189
Chocolate Pancake Dessert	35
Chop Suey	168
Chuchurbawang	55
Clam Canapés	60
Clam Dip	61
Cocktail or Tea Puffs	19
Cocktail Tid Bits	63
Corn Pie	17
Cottage Cheese Ham Rolls	88
Cottage Cheese Pancakes	34
Cottage Cheese Paneer Spread	105
Cottage Cheese Snacks	106
Creamcheese Pie (II)	21
Criss Cross Linzer	22
Crumb-Fried or Batter-Fried Cottage Cheese	101
Crumb-Fried or Batter-Fried Roe	98
Czech Apple Strűdel	37
Czech Fritters	25
Dalia or Borgul Malpua (Cracked Wheat Pancakes)	36
Dalia Pakora (Cracked Wheat or Borgul Balls)	71
Dalia Porridge	187
Dárazsfeszek – (Hungarian Sweet Pastry)	39
Delicious Creamcheese Pie (I)	20
Dessert Sauces	131
Donut	24
Dosa (South Indian Stuffed Pancakes)	152
Easy Brown Sauce	126

Recipe	Page
Egg Kebab	77
Egyptian Kabeba	78
Falafel	69
Feijoada Paulista (Brazilian Dish)	145
Finnish Cabbage Pie	158
Fish Katchuri	109
Fish Wafers	99
Flaky Pastry	10
Flavoured Cottage/Cream Cheese On Toast	103
Fruit Waffles/Fritters/Pancakes	38
Fuyong Hai (Indonesian)	171
German Apple Fritters	26
Glögg (Swedish Hot Christmas Drink)	143
Gooseberry Jam (I)	114
Gooseberry Jam (II)	115
Granola	188
Ground Meat, Chicken or Fish Pie	182
Guava Cheese	120
Guava Jelly	119
Guava Pie	30
Guyanese Rich Coconut Bens	44
Hungarian Savoury Dish	150
Idli or South Indian Steam-Buns	151
Indian Black Berry (Kaala Jaam) Tart	29
Indonesian Spring Rolls The Easy Way	164
Japanese Beans Rolled in Pork	51

Recipe	Page
Kanchkala or Green Banana Burgers	83
Karelian Steak	159
Katjang Mana Lagi (Indonesian Peanut Brittle)	73
Kharisa (Assamese Bamboo Shoot Pickle)	136
Khasta Fish Puffs	107
Khasta Singara	110
Koubbeh (Lebanese National Dish)	160
Lahmedjun (Armenian Pizzas)	97
Lahnmahajan or Lebanese Pizza	95
Langosh	40
Left-Over From Left-Overs!	175
Lemon Ginger Juice	122
Liver and Pork Paté	68
Liver Paté	67
Luncheon Meat Koftas	75
Methi (Fenugreek) Straws	52
Mince Kebabs	76
Mock Cream	129
Mock Lasagne	185
Mock Sour Cream	130
Mowcha (Banana Flower) Kebabs	82
Mowcha or Banana Flower Koftas	80
Mummy's Vindaloo or Meat Pickle	138
Olive and Bacon Canapés	62
Oopuma (Savoury Semolina Dish from South India)	172
Oriental Meat Loaf	169

Recipe	Page
Pakhlava	13
Pancake Party	147
Peanut Butter	121
Pear Jam	116
Phyllo or Filo Pastry (Middle Eastern)	9
Pineapple Jam (I)	117
Pineapple Jam (II)	118
Pineapple Squash	124
Piquant Sausages	89
Placky or Czech Savory Potato Pancakes	59
Pork Pickle	137
Potato Crisps	53
Prawn Snacks	100
Preserved Potatoes Chips	54
Preserving Vegetables	176
Quick and Easy Pizza	184
Quick Economic Apple Pancakes	27
Quick Hamburgers	183
Quick Kebabs or Koftas	79
Quick White Sauce	125
Radish Flower	177
Recycling Left-Over Tandoori Roti or Chapattis	157
Rempejek* (Indonesian Peanut Chips)	74
Rice Cakes or Pakoras	72
Rolls From Left-Over Mince Curry	86
Sago Bhujia	50
Salad Platter	180
Salty Biscuits	93

Recipe	Page
Sangria (I)	141
Sausage Rolls	84
Savory Peanut Biscuits	92
Savory Sesame Machine Biscuits	91
Savoury Biscuits	94
Savoury Rolls	87
Scrambled Cabbage with Left-Over Meat	174
Semolina Dosa (South Indian Pancakes)	154
Simple Quick Easy Orange Marmalade	113
South Indian Lassi	144
Soya Bean Pie	32
Spinach Pie	18
Spring Rolls (I)	161
Stuffed Batter Fried Patal/Palwal (Indian Vegetable)	178
Stuffed Dill Pickle	64
Sukiyaki	170
Surprise Potatoes	56
Sushi	166
Tahina Sauce (Middle Eastern)	127
Tamagodofu (Japanese)	167
Tomato Chutney	135
Tomato Purée	134
Wood Apple (Baël) Squash	123
Yorkshire Pudding	12

www.ingramcontent.com/pod-product-compliance
Lightning Source LLC
LaVergne TN
LVHW061611070526
838199LV00078B/7243